What Others Are Saying About *F*

"Jim Jenkins speaks to the founda[...] today. The relativism, humanism, and diminishing regard for the authority of God's Word, along with the paucity of pulpits where the Scriptures are exegeted faithfully and expounded with boldness, has laid the soul of the 21st century church open to immense risk. I heartily encourage pastors, and any others who care about Christ's people and our needy world, to read this book. I am particularly grateful for its boldness and faithfulness to speak with passion, while avoiding the condescending, stentorian tone too often sounded when addressing such a needful message."

DR. JACK HAYFORD
CHANCELLOR OF THE KING'S UNIVERSITY, LOS ANGELES CA

"Jim Jenkins has written a powerful exposé of the spiritual illness afflicting many evangelical churches today over the nature of Scripture. Out of a rich background in several ministries over a span of several decades, Jim writes with clarity, precision, and integrity. His use of metaphors, including those drawn from the sea, enriches his treatment and shows just how dark and foreboding the uncharted waters are. All who care for the 'ship' of the church should read his book."

DR. JAMES DE YOUNG
AUTHOR OF *BURNING DOWN THE SHACK*

"In this postmodern culture, which suggests our scientific age is old and we need a new, culturally relevant way to reach this new age, it is important that we take time to focus on what Francis Schaffer called 'true truth.' We need to be reminded that, historically, belief systems and knowledge continue to change, but truth is timeless and never changes. Also, the God who created man in His own image and likeness is able and has communicated with His creation. Dr. Jim Jenkins has effectively communicated that the truth of God's inerrant Word to modern man in our generation is reliable and worthy of our trust and faith."

PAUL SMITH
AUTHOR OF *NEW EVANGELICALISM: NEW WORLD ORDER*

"It is a pleasure to endorse Dr. Jim Jenkins, a trusted colleague and former student. His passion for the Word of God springs from every page. He says, 'Throughout my entire ministry I have been watching, warning, and preaching because I see something. There has been a steady, methodical, relentless assault on the authority of the Scriptures' (p. 74). The postmodern reaction against all propositional truth, especially in the Bible, exacerbates this assault and further erodes the authority of the Bible.

I applaud Jim's outrage! With skilled writing and a kindly tone, he shows us the dangers we face. I urge every spiritual leader and pastor to read this book. It will open your eyes to the tragedy of calibrating our message to the culture, instead of the proclaiming the timeless principles of the Word of God."

DR. RONALD E. COTTLE
FOUNDER-PRESIDENT OF CHRISTIAN LIFE EDUCATORS NETWORK;
ACTS NETWORK

"It's not too late! A deadly drift toward popular trends threatens theological truths. Navigating the rugged shoreline of the pounding Pacific Northwest, this former Navy chaplain boldly warns of impending doom. With vivid illustrations of the sea, Jim graphically describes the subtle spiritual situations that must be reversed. Perhaps this treasure will ignite revival in our day. Jonathan Edwards penned these words: "From the beginning of time, God has had revival on His mind."

DR. RALPH WILKERSON
FOUNDER OF THE MELODYLAND SCHOOL OF THEOLOGY;
PASTOR OF MELODYLAND CHRISTIAN CENTER.

"Jim Jenkins proclaims the clarion call that challenges today's believers to remember that the Holy Bible is not just an ordinary book, but one divinely inspired by the Almighty God. The theology of today's evangelicals is being called into question by the media, progressives, and college professors; today's scientific, intellectual, and political negativism toward the Bible has spilled over into the classroom where young students are chastised for defending their faith. *Fatal Drift* is thorough and biblically sound; it is a comprehensive read that penetrates to the core of the problem evangelicals face today—compromise. Jim Jenkins calls on every believer to return to the faith of our fathers, who proclaimed the plenary inspiration of Scripture—to become apologists in the face of progressivism as it forges onward. Every Christian should read Jenkins' book. It will make a difference in their lives."

DR. HENRY HARBUCK
INTERNATIONAL OVERSEER OF THE ASSOCIATION OF
EVANGELICAL GOSPEL MINISTRIES;
GENERAL EDITOR OF THE *NEW MILLENNIA IN-DEPTH BIBLE*

FATAL DRIFT

DR. JIM JENKINS

FATAL DRIFT

Is the Church Losing Its Anchor?

Deep River
BOOKS

ISBN – 13: 9781940269306
ISBN – 10: 194026930X
Library of Congress: 2014950249

Printed in the USA

Cover design by David Litwin

ACKNOWLEDGMENTS

To Dr. Victor Gardner, founding president of The Foursquare Gospel Church of Canada, whose example and godly character helped shape a young pastor who had more zeal than sense, I am eternally grateful. He did not surrender to trendiness or rely on the human potential of his charges nearly so much as modeled for us all what it meant to be a person totally reliant on the guidance of the Holy Spirit.

To Holly Jenkins, whose steady attention to detail helped me to edit the text and control my preacher's penchant for hyperbole, I am greatly indebted. My son married well.

To Pastor Larry R. Johnson… The church growth researchers will not write about his statistics, but his exploits for the Kingdom of God surely have not escaped the Father's notice. From the day we were ordained into the ministry in 1978, Pastor Larry has not ceased to faithfully preach the Word, comfort the sick, and care for his community. I am honored to call him my friend. Many of the insights recorded in this book are the result of my interactions with him over the years.

To my wife, Judy, I owe a great debt. She put up with a lot over thirty-three years of public ministry. Every church we served was made stronger due to her steady, behind-the-scenes leadership. A consummate musician, she has enriched the lives of all her students, and has had a great deal of influence at the local high school choir music programs. Our children and now our grandchildren serve the Lord because of Judy's example.

Finally, I dedicate this book to my sister Joan Talley. She has been an anchor bolt in my life. Her steady, dogged determination to follow Jesus, her quick wit and her courage in the face of adversity have served to inspire all those who have been privileged to have known her. When I grow up, I want to be more like her.

CONTENTS

Introduction 13

1. Near the Watershed 17

2. From the Watershed to Cape Disappointment 31

3. Where's the Runaway Lane? 45

4. About Bridges 55

5. "You Eyeballed It, Didn't You?" 61

6. About The Trustworthiness of Instruments 83

7. Conforming to the Cross or
    Calibrating to the Culture? 91

8. Compass Calls and Counter-Information 101

9. Two Clicks Away: The Lost Art of Vetting 113

10. From TIME to TIME 121

11. The Church Must Speak Out 139

12. It Could Happen Here 149

13. The Offense of the Cross 161

14. Anybody Seen a Trumpet? 173

Epilogue 193

Notes 201

Bibliography 215

INTRODUCTION

I wasn't raised reading the Bible. In fact I didn't own one until I was in my twenties. I was raised by parents who believed in the God of the Bible and saw to it that we went to church and learned our religion. They were devout Catholics who taught us right from wrong and instilled in each of us a deep sense of personal responsibility. They were not perfect. Clearly my siblings and I weren't perfect either. But my folks did the best they could with the knowledge they had, and for their tenacity and faithfulness, I am eternally grateful.

In the early 1970s, at the height of what is now called the Jesus Movement, I had a dynamic encounter with God. I was born again. God sovereignly reached down, got my attention, and led me to a church where everybody had a Bible. I remember my first Bible. I even remember how the pages smelled. I read it so much the glue of the binding gave way and whole chapters would fall out.

Throughout the decades that followed, I have owned dozens of Bibles, but that first one still sits on a shelf in my library. Every time I see it, I am reminded of God's great love and his unmerited favor extended to such a sinner as me. I came across this quote in the devotional *Streams in The Desert* that best describes how I feel.

There is no commentator of the Scriptures half so valuable as a captivity. The old Psalms have quavered for us with a new pathos as we sat by our "Babel's Stream" and have sounded for us with new joy as we found our captivity turned to the streams in the south.

The man who has seen much affliction will not readily part with his copy of the Word of God. Another book may seem to others to be identical with his own, but to him it is not the same, for over his old and tearstained Bible he has written, in characters visible to no eyes but his own, the record of his experiences, and ever and anon he comes on Bethel pillars, or Elim Palms, which are to him the memorials of some critical chapters in his history.[1]

This book is about not only what my Bible has meant to me, but also what has happened to the trustworthiness of the Bible in my generation. The Jesus Movement was in many ways a Bible-based phenomenon. I was not the only new believer who had little or no familiarity with the Bible. Perhaps that is why I am loath to take liberties with it. Frankly, I am still in awe of the fact that God has given us His Word in written form. To treat it as mere literature is to me obscene.

One of the very first lessons I learned in my newfound faith was that God still speaks today, and the way to discern if it is really Him speaking is to search the Bible and see if He has spoken about the issue in question in the Scriptures.

Once I became spiritually alive and aware that I was now in relationship with God, the Bible became a lifeline for me. In fact, the way I learned about my newfound relationship with God was itself found in its pages. It never occurred to me to doubt its trustworthiness or truthfulness. When I came across a passage I didn't understand, or one I thought was a little odd, I with childlike trust assumed that one day the Lord would clear up any confusion. He would do that by revealing the answer... in the Bible.

It was when I was called by the Lord to train for public ministry that the whole issue of the inerrancy of the Bible first came to my attention. As I prayed about which seminary to attend and as I researched a number of them, it became clear to me that not every institution held the belief that the Bible was inerrant.

Thankfully, my pastor was on the board of regents of a brand new theological school in Southern California. They forthrightly declared that they were looking for people who would apply themselves to scholarship, but ultimately submit themselves to the guidance of the Holy Spirit. Their statement of faith about the inerrancy of Scripture was unambiguous.[2] The faculty was comprised of leading scholars and authors who were not only highly competent and proficient in their individual disciplines, but were also committed to an inerrant Bible and the belief that the Holy Spirit could take the Words of God and make precise application in every area of life.

The Bibles I have used over the years have reflected my journey of faith. Some are scholarly editions, designed for and used by seminary students. Still others are so-called "Study Bibles" meant for devotional use and edification. I even have a few Bibles with desert camouflage covers. These are treasured mementos of my days as a military chaplain.

Some of my paperback Bibles are dog-eared. Some are ornate and bound with expensive leather. I even have a Gideon Bible that I "borrowed" from a hotel. Some have been given to me as gifts. Some were given to me by family members to use as I conducted the funeral of a dear saint who passed away. I would use the margin notes from that person's Bible as part of my message.

Virtually all of my Bibles are marked up with notes in the margin, coats of yellow highlighter bleeding through the paper, question marks, exclamation points, and even a few primitive cartoons. The Bible has been the main source that informed my preaching, my counseling, and my care of the flocks I served. My prayers have always been filled with verses of Scripture.

During three decades of public ministry I have seen a disturbing trend develop. As the church has become more and more secular, the Bible is becoming less and less the primary source of preaching and teaching. The phrase "the Bible says" is being replaced by phrases like "The most recent polls suggest… " or "Oprah says" or "A recent study has shown… "

Preaching propositional truth has given way to "conversations" which are designed to promote ambiguity and a studied lack of certainty. Apologetics has devolved into apologies. Without even realizing that they have done it, many preachers have actually come into agreement with an ancient enemy by mouthing, in one way or another, the same question he asked in the garden, "And hath God *truly* said?"

This book represents my conviction that the abandonment of the doctrine of inerrancy of Scripture has brought about a perilous situation. I remember a TIME magazine cover that showed a page of The United States Constitution halfway through a paper shredder. The title on the magazine's cover read, "Does it Still Matter?" As I stared at it I thought, "That could just as easily be the first page of Genesis, and the same question could be asked of synods and seminaries, preachers, and parishioners."

Drawing upon illustrations gleaned from a lifetime of pastoral ministry, a twenty-year career as a Navy Reserve chaplain, and a decade as a Bible College professor, I hope my experiences will serve to underscore the importance of inerrancy. I mean to tackle this issue head on.

A.B. Simpson once said:

> God is looking for men on whom He can put the weight of all His love and power and faithful promises. God's engines are strong enough to draw any weight we attach to them. Unfortunately the cable which we fasten to the engine is often too weak to hold the weight of our prayer. Therefore God is drilling us, disciplining us to stability and certainty in the life of faith. Let us learn our lessons and stand fast.[3]

Is it important that any discussion of inerrancy has all but disappeared from our seminaries? Is it a significant development that today many pastors doubt that whole passages of Scripture were inspired? Do we need to accommodate the culture or confront it?

These questions beg answers. I have already experienced the rebukes of some who feel that this book represents an overreaction on my part, and that it really doesn't matter whether the Bible is inerrant. I respectfully disagree. Frankly, I believe it is the defining issue of our times.

In the pages that follow, it is my earnest prayer that you, dear reader, will come to see why it matters.

ONE

NEAR THE WATERSHED

It was in Salmon Arm, British Columbia. I was involved with starting a church in a beautiful mountain community not far from the headwaters of the mighty Columbia River.

Being a new church (we met in a rented movie theater) I opted to rent an office in the same building as the local newspaper. I felt that there I could get my finger on the pulse of the community. One day, I had the radio on and heard an announcement that at noon there was to be a ceremony held at the veterans' memorial. They were going to plant a "Peace Pole," whatever that was, and it was all connected somehow to the United Nations. I was intrigued and walked the few blocks to the memorial.

A large group of people were holding hands in a wide circle, swaying and chanting something. I inched closer and heard,

We'd rather be dancing than marching. We'd rather hold hands than a gun. We are the New Age begun and we're learning the dance one by one.[1]

What I saw and heard that day got my attention. The ideology articulated at that ceremony has, over the decades that have followed, developed into an agenda that has rapidly influenced not only the culture, but has infiltrated the church as well. The marriage of progressive politics and progressive religion was being fleshed out right before my eyes.

In 1984 Francis Schaeffer predicted that if the slide away from orthodoxy that he chronicled in *The Great Evangelical Disaster* continued, it was inevitable that one day there would come a time when a system would be introduced which would offer a solution to the world's woes. It would involve accommodation to the prevailing world spirit, which would entail some measure of collusion between disparate groups and subtle deception, and in the end, result in an outright abandonment of Christianity as we know it. What I saw that day in a town not far from the watershed of the Columbia River was much more than it initially seemed.

Fast forward to 2012. I look back to that day in Canada and now realize that I was witnessing something that had implications far beyond a quirky New Age demonstration. Things proposed that day would, as they were slowly and methodically implemented, have profound effects on the culture for decades to come.

What appeared to be nebulous speculative philosophical musings now have become much more precise and in some instances even enacted into law. New Age spirituality has now gained a hearing at heretofore conservative seminaries. The Green movement, using the United Nation's checkbook, is aggressively pushing a sustainability policy, which is becoming increasingly anti-Christian in North America and around the world.

Here is what I saw that day. The people swaying in the circle were activists from various agencies who had a core set of beliefs in common. These were folks who embraced the notion that the only solution to the world's problems was a "one-world" government. This entity would need to be based on so-called "one-world" spirituality. The local Salmon Arm newspaper coverage of the event contained the following description of the goals of one particular organization that was funded by the UN, which sponsored the Peace Pole planting.

> The goals of The World Peace University are to educate people who desire to create a world where peace is a way of life, where environmental balance exists, where there is food sufficiency, where social justice prevails and where an individual achieves the highest degree of self-realization within a community of co-operation.[2]

Sounds good, doesn't it? Sounds familiar too. This is because today a group of progressive Christians who call themselves the Emergent Church is using similar, in some cases identical, language to describe its goals. Their philosophy/theology entails a shift away from emphasizing propositional truth and the teaching of systematic theology to an emphasis on service to humanity—things like eliminating hunger, establishing social justice, etc. There is an intentional shift away from a "dominion over creation" stance to a more "green" eco-friendly, sustainable, cooperative model. One Christian university in Oregon now offers a degree program with a concentration in "Earth Keeping."[3]

Back to Salmon Arm… Once the group completed their Sacred Circle Dance they transitioned into the rest of the program. Some of the participants gathering there that week were the Canadian Ambassador to the UN, one of the founders of the National Audubon Society's Expedition Institute, and the former head of Radio Moscow.

A teen-aged girl got up and recited a manifesto of sorts. I was stunned when she reached the point in her address where she, in a matter-of-fact fashion said, "All religions that are not harmonious with the New Age must be eliminated.…"

They proceeded to erect the Peace Pole in a ceremony which I learned later had previously taken place in other cities around the world. It was part of a UN initiative.

For all of its language about peace and harmony, this was in fact the beginning of a methodical scheme to gain control over natural resources. This in turn would result in an enormous wealth-generating machine controlled by a coalition of ambitious self-appointed leaders who envision a one-world government. I will have more to say about this when I discuss Canadian billionaire Maurice Strong, Al Gore, Bill Clinton, and others involved in the money-for-carbon offset credits scam.

Fliers were disseminated advertising something called "The World Peace University Society." In the weeks that followed, I did a little research. I learned that many of the community groups in our little town had the same individuals serving on their boards as directors. From day care facilities to youth initiatives to recreation programs to community colleges, these same people were part of a group called the World Peace University Society.

I wrote a letter to the editor of the local paper in which I commented on the ceremony. I questioned the agenda of this organization and its New Age affiliations. I received a letter in reply. The director of the World Peace University Society was taking issue with my characterization of the goals of his organization.

Listed on the stationery was the board of directors—a "who's who" of New Age celebrities. As I did more research, I found links to a man named Maurice Strong, a one-world government proponent who was then angling to become the next Canadian Ambassador to the UN. Notables involved with the Peace University Society included Canada's current UN Ambassador, Steven Lewis, Hollywood actor Dennis Weaver, and a group called "Lucis Trust."[4]

Lucis Trust caught my eye. I learned that the name of this organization had been changed so as not to alarm people. The original name was Lucifer Publishing and it was a major player in the early days of the New Age movement.

Once I began to publicly question these things, I received another letter from the World Peace University. I noticed that the stationery looked almost identical to the first letter I received. Looking more closely I discovered that Lucis Trust had been removed (scrubbed) from the list of the board of directors shortly after my letter to the editor appeared in which I had pointed out the Lucis Trust connection.

Without going into too much detail, suffice it to say, I was alarmed. The next development hit closer to home. One day, not that long after the Peace Pole ceremony, my daughter Hannah came home with a strange look on her face.

"What happened, honey? Anything wrong?"

"Oh, something happened at school today. We had a substitute teacher. After recess, we were all kind of hyper and he did something that scared me. He had us all put our heads down. He turned out the lights and began to tell us how to breathe. Then he played this strange music. Telling us how to breathe, he said, "Don't be alarmed, some of you may see a beautiful woman appear.... This is Gaia.... I was scared, Dad, and I wouldn't close my eyes."[5]

I drove immediately to the school, walked past the secretary, and past the principal into the classroom. I saw the substitute and found the cassette recorder. I popped out the cassette and said, "I'll be right back."

I drove to the local New Age bookstore and went to the music section and there, lo and behold, was the cassette this teacher had used. The jacket actually said, "These are the subliminal messages you will receive." They all had to do with harmony and nature and Gaia worship.

I went back to the school and confronted the principal. He swore that the substitute acted alone and that had he known he would never have allowed it. Spurred on by this incident, I then broadened my research into the school curriculum in BC.

The annual Provincial Convention of School Trustees (the Canadian equivalent of our Superintendents of Schools) that year had scheduled as their plenary speaker a woman from the Meta Intelligence Institute in North Carolina. Her topic was "Advancing New Age Children into the Next Millennium." I wrote a letter of protest and received a reply that said:

> Dr. Mr. Jenkins,
> You clearly misunderstood the intent of our proposed presenter.
> But enough of you wrote that we have decided to cancel our presentation.

I could almost hear the theme music from *The Twilight Zone*. Was this really happening? Had I entered some sort of evil vortex? Was I low on blood sugar?

Toward the end of this sequence of events, a man from my church came to me and took me aside in a cloak-and-dagger sort of way. He worked in a local bank. He was actually afraid. In hushed tones he said, "You did not hear this from me. Is that clear?"

He went on to say, "You have no idea who you are fooling with. There is an enormous amount of UN money being funneled into this town. This is all much larger than you can imagine."

Looking deeper, I studied Canada's involvement with the UN and learned of another interesting group, The World Economic Forum which meets in Davos, Switzerland.[6] I discovered why my friend was afraid. The politicians and activists talking about globalism and one-world spirituality were not fringe characters at all. These were well-funded political heavyweights. This seemingly obscure group in a small town in BC was part of a much larger group with an agenda that would one day affect us all.

In 2014 the fusion of progressive politics and progressive religion appears to be about to reach critical mass. Many of the early New Age beliefs embraced by the Sacred Circle dancers in Salmon Arm are considered mainstream Emergent Church practice now.

Have you noticed the explosive growth of the number of "spiritual formation" programs at seminaries? Look into the content of those programs. Vet the authors of the texts. Would anyone back in the eighties have believed that in a mere thirty-year period Christians would be encouraged to walk labyrinths and practice deep relaxation techniques and breathing techniques... "to empty their minds"?[7]

Paul Smith, the brother of Chuck Smith, founder of Calvary Chapel, in his book, *New Evangelicalism: The New World Order* makes an observation that is especially germane to our discussion of how things have deteriorated so rapidly:

Satan knows that to bring about his plan for the world he must capture man's mind by influencing what man believes to be true. The Bible teaches that what we think determines who we are (Prov. 23:7). How we look at life determines how we live our life. Peoples' view about truth also determines how they interpret the Bible. Social scientists think that if you can control a person's concept of truth, you can control that person..."[8]

Smith cites Francis Schaeffer:

(Schaeffer) emphasized that biblical truth is stated in propositional form; in words that can be understood by all mankind. The basic problem with philosophy, sociology and anthropology in academia is that it begins with man; and man has no inherent capacity to discern truth because he is in a spiritually fallen state.[9]

Paul Smith makes this bold assessment:

Postmodernism is a tool of Satan which has lured away the new evangelicals causing them to fabricate an Emergent Church. The fabric of New Evangelicalism consists of many threads: Fuller Seminary, Peter Drucker, Bob Buford, Rick Warren are tightly woven together, and they want to go global, but with the social gospel instead of the good news described in the New Testament.[10]

He adds,

Emergent church leader Leonard Sweet is often quoted in Warren's Ministry Tool Box.

Sweet says, "A sea change of transitions and transformations is birthing a whole new world… Postmodern culture is a change-or-be-changed world… reinvent yourself for the twenty-first century or die… some would rather die than change.[11]

As I read these simple bold statements, I was struck by how refreshingly blunt they appeared in contrast with all the nebulous, intentionally ambiguous material I have come across in some of the blogs that deal with the Emergent Church conversation.

An article by Warren B. Smith (no relation to Paul Smith as far as I know) is equally provocative, "Are Christian and Emerging Leaders Heading Toward a False Christ Through Quantum Spirituality?"

Many prominent New Age figures have stated that the foundational teaching of The New World Religion is the "immanence of God" (i.e. God "in" everything). Benjamin Crème, New Age leader and spokesperson for the false New Age Christ, Maitreya, says:

But eventually a new world religion will be inaugurated which will be a fusion and synthesis of the approach of the East and the approach of The West. The Christ will bring together not simply Christianity and Buddhism, but the concept of God transcendent (outside his creation)—and also of God immanent (in man and all creation.)[12]

Warren Smith shows how this premise from New Age religion has found its way into the writings of Emergent thinkers like Leonard Sweet. Author of *The Tao of Physics*, Frijof Capra, describes the union of mysticism and the new physics as the new spirituality that is now being developed by many groups and movements both inside and outside the churches. As an example of how this "new spirituality" is moving into the church, he refers to one of Leonard Sweet's role models and heroes, Matthew Fox (Fox is a defrocked Catholic Priest.)

On the other hand, I also believe that our own spiritual traditions will have to undergo some radical changes to harmonize with the values of the new paradigm. The spirituality corresponding to the new vision of reality I have been outlining here is likely to be an ecological, earth-oriented, post-patriarchal spirituality…an example would be the creation-centered spirituality promoted by Matthew Fox and his colleagues.'"[13]

Warren Smith shows that there is a definite linkage to this line of thinking and the positions held by emerging thinkers who convene at the Leadership Network conventions.

At their May 2000 Exploring Off the Map Conference with Leonard Sweet and others, Margaret Wheatley describes how she first encountered the "new science" in Capra's book, *The Turning Point:*

I opened my first book on the "new science," Fritjof Capra's *The Turning Point* which describes the new world view emerging from quantum physics. This provided my first glimpse of a new way of perceiving the world, one that comprehended its processes of change, its deeply patterned nature, and its dense webs of connections.[14]

To further illustrate how pervasive this quantum spirituality has become, consider an organization called "Vantage Point 3." This group has developed a three-phase "spiritual formation" program called the "Vantage Point 3 Process"...which incidentally is being used by a growing number of churches across North America.

In the first phase (called) "Emerging Leaders," a quote and a summation of Margaret Wheatley is used to teach one of the points in that phase. The curriculum quotes Wheatley from her book *Leadership and the New Science* and emphasizes her view on relationship and interconnection.

Smith rightly concluded,

Wheatley's quantum Christ is the Universal Christ of quantum oneness. Vantage Point 3's use of Wheatley to teach about "Christ" is a perfect example of what Frijof Capra described as "the new spirituality being developed within the churches."[15]

I know how fringe-like this all sounds. I would have dismissed it had I not stumbled on to the Peace Pole ceremony in Canada all those years ago. I put it to the reader. Do you see any similarity between Frijof Capra's content and the UN initiative birthed in Canada? Capra's remarks displayed against the backdrop of the Peace Pole ceremony are chilling:

I also believe that our own spiritual traditions will have to undergo some radical changes to harmonize with the values of the new paradigm. The spirituality corresponding to the new vision of reality I have been outlining here is likely to be an ecological, earth oriented, post-patriarchal spirituality.[16]

Think back to the description of the mission of the World Peace University which cites the "desire to create a world where peace is a way of life, where environmental balance exists, where there is food sufficiency, where social justice prevails and where an individual achieves the highest degree of self-realization within a community of co-operation."

It adds a definite eerie tone to Capra's statement that "Our own spiritual traditions will have to undergo some radical changes."

Back to what I learned in Canada. When I researched the New Age agenda, I noticed that references to the World Economic Forum, which meets annually in Davos, Switzerland, were popping up in a lot of the literature. People like Maurice Strong, George Soros, and other one-world types would meet to discuss how to implement the new order of things.

Fox News has this to say about Maurice Strong:

Controversy, along with radical environmental and economic views, is what Strong has long been known for. He took up residence in Beijing in 2005, after serving as the UN 's special envoy to North Korea, when investigators of the Oil for Food scandal uncovered the fact that he had cashed a check for nearly $1 million from Tongsun Park, a South Korean political fixer who was later convicted of conspiring to bribe UN officials on behalf of Iraqi dictator Saddam Hussein.

Strong was never accused of any wrongdoing, and said his move to China at that time was no more than a coincidence. Since then, Strong, an avowed life-long socialist, has been engaged, in low-key fashion, in a number of business deals involving the Chinese government.

He also served as a director of the Chicago Climate Exchange, one of the first attempts to create a commercial cap-and-trade market in the US. Recently, he has also taken part in preliminary walk-up meetings for Rio + 20 in China, though without official title.[17] Giving Strong one last star turn on a UN environmental stage, despite his past brushes with scandal, is an interesting gambit for the UN, though it has apparently approached the matter cautiously. The fact is that Strong is the closest thing to global environmentalism's patron saint— or, to conservative critics, the foremost gray eminence of the movement to expand "global environmental governance"— which is once more on the international agenda at Rio + 20."[18]

The Wall Street Journal's Claudia Rosett interviewed Strong in October 2008. Her piece gives us few more interesting facts about Strong:

I have been waiting a long time to ask a further question, prompted by evidence that emerged in the Tongsun Park trial, showing that three years after delivering that Baghdad-funded check to Mr. Strong, Park was transferring money directly into Mr. Strong's personal bank account to pay the rent for a private office maintained by Mr. Strong in midtown Manhattan. Why was Mr. Park paying Mr. Strong's office rent? "He was paying his own rent," replies Mr. Strong, adding that the arrangement was a "sublet." "I had the UN office, so I didn't really need all that space... he wanted an address in New York."

But there were signs that the same premises were also used at some point as a New York office by the UN-chartered University for Peace (a small school headquartered in Costa Rica, which with Mr. Strong chairing its board from 1999-2006 developed an out-sized interest in proposing UN-funded development projects for North Korea, and used UN facilities to arrange trips for North Korean officials to Europe). What was that about? It was only "interim," says Mr. Strong. "It was a motley office."

(The UN-chartered University for Peace is none other than the World Peace University Society—rebranded and relocated to Costa Rica [author's comment]).

He grows irritable that I am "resurrecting all this." He talks much more cheerfully about his current projects. He says he is still Canadian, keeps a home in Canada, and pays taxes there. But most of his work right now is in China. His erratic health leaves him less interested in global travel. He says he suffers from diabetes, and has had five heart bypasses: "I have a cow's valve in my heart."[19]

Follow the dots. Maurice Strong is a billionaire, due in no small part to his insider status in the Green movement. He owns the rights to some of the largest aquifers in North America. He lives in China, now lobbying the Chinese about issues like carbon offset revenues. Does that concept sound familiar?

Al Gore, another frequent participant at the World Economic Forum, addressed the group at Davos in 2008. His topic? "A Unified Earth Theory." The Nobel Prize winner is at the forefront of the cash-for-carbon offset scheme that is gaining momentum every year.

Recently joining the likes of Maurice Strong, George Soros, Al Gore, and Bono at Davos are newcomers Rick Warren and now, Emergent Church leader Brian McClaren. It is extremely troublesome to see prominent "Christian" leaders who are at the table with others who have long since made their desire for a one-world government based on a homogenized one-world spirituality crystal clear.

Maurice Strong has strong ties (pun intended) with the New Age Movement. A Google search of "Maurice Strong and New Age Spirituality" will yield a few days' worth of interesting research. My purpose in citing all of this is to point out that Strong, Gore, Soros, and others are all on record as supporting a one-world governance; which in turn must rely on a change of consciousness that will lead the masses of people to embrace a New Age spirituality with Luciferian roots.

Strong in particular has been actively promoting UN initiatives that focus on "educating toward a consciousness" that will result in the masses embracing "one-world spirituality." In order for those initiatives to succeed, there must be, as the teenager in Salmon Arm announced over twenty years ago, "The elimination of all religions that are not harmonious with the New Age."

Make your own conclusions about what I just shared, but what I hope to do in this book is to show that this kind of confusion and intrigue can only be possible in a climate in which the Bible has been devalued.

Spurgeon called it *The Great Down Grade*. Francis Schaeffer called it *The Great Evangelical Disaster*. Harold Lindsell, cofounder of *Christianity Today*, dubbed it *The Battle for the Bible*. I believe that this debate in the history of the church recurs for a reason.

The namesake of Lucis Trust, Lucifer, has never hidden his tactics. His was a clear challenge to both the integrity of God's Word and the capacity of humans to trust its veracity and authority. It should come as no surprise that the enemy of our souls would try in every generation to get the people of God to distrust, or in some instances discard, the parts of the Word of God they don't like.

What does all of this have to do with the inerrancy of the Bible? Consider the following:

- In order to fuse progressive politics and progressive religion, the "troublesome" passages which state that Christ is the only way of salvation in the Bible have to be dealt with.
- One effective way is to redefine the gospel from salvation found in Christ alone to a kinder/gentler version—more akin to global religious initiatives to feed the poor and solve the environmental crises that seem to be plaguing the planet with increasing frequency and severity.
- To change the Christian culture, changes in emphasis must take place in seminaries and Bible Schools. Back away from any notion of certainty and exclusivity to do with the claims of Christ and begin to talk in inclusive, pluralistic terms like Quantum Spirituality and Earth Keeping.
- Above all else do not confront the culture. Do not talk about humans as sinners needing a savior. Speak in terms of potential earth changers who need to understand that god is in all religions and in all beings.

No one who believes that the Bible is inerrant would even entertain New Age spirituality, for the Bible contains clear indictments against those who entertain such syncretistic, and in some instances, overtly pagan practices.

In this book I will chronicle what I see as the abdication of the church in the face of the barrage of progressive indoctrination. It is now the exception rather than the rule to find a seminary that holds its faculty to a rigid adherence to the doctrine of inerrancy. Consequently we have pastors and leaders who are confused at best, and manipulated at worst when it comes to a definitive position on the issue of inerrancy.

I reject the notion that it is somehow noble to explore alternatives when the Lord says we are to avoid them.[20] I have heard the argument, "We have knowledge that the first-century Christians didn't have."

Do we have a different Jesus?

This is not some petty squabble over semantics. It is not a case of hipsters versus boomers. It is, in point of fact, about the eternal destiny of souls.

It matters.

Two

FROM THE
WATERSHED TO
CAPE DISAPPOINTMENT

The snow lies along that watershed, unbroken as a seeming unity.
But when it melts, where it ends in its destination is literally thousands of miles apart. That is a watershed. That is what a watershed
is. A watershed divides. A clear line can be drawn between what
seems at first to be the same or at least very close, but in reality
ends in different situations. A watershed is a line. Evangelicals today
are facing a watershed concerning the nature of biblical inspiration
and authority…like the snow lying side by side on the ridge, the
new views on biblical authority often seem at first glance not to be
so very far from what evangelicals, until just recently, have always
believed. But also, like the snow lying side by side on the ridge, the
two views when followed consistently end up a thousand miles
apart.

FRANCIS SCHAEFFER

The church I pastored in British Columbia was located not far from
the headwaters of the Columbia River. At its source the Columbia
River is really not much more than a creek one could easily walk
across. In the spectacular Rocky Mountains of BC, this trickle makes some
critical turns that have shaped the lives of millions.

In its over 1,200-mile journey to the sea, the bends and grades along
its confluence with other rivers gives the river exponential power to shape
the landscape. The Columbia River Gorge, which separates Washington
State from Oregon, is a prime example. The same power that carves gorges
through solid rock can also make for dangerous conditions for mariners.
Listen to this description of the place where the Columbia joins the sea:

The Columbia empties into the Pacific Ocean just west of Astoria, Oregon, over the Columbia Bar, a shifting sandbar that makes the river's mouth one of the most hazardous stretches of water to navigate in the world. Because of the danger and the many shipwrecks near the mouth, it acquired a reputation as the "Graveyard of Ships."[1]

The same powerful force that lights and warms millions of homes, water, is also capable of causing shipwrecks and disaster, and it all starts at the watershed. It is interesting that the reason it is so dangerous is a shifting sandbar.

In 1984 (how ironic is that) Francis Schaeffer released *The Great Evangelical Disaster.* I gave it a cursory read and passed it off as perhaps a bit too extreme and alarmist in tone. His very title was, I thought at the time, judgmental and combative. Now as I read his prophetic warning, I repent of my judgmental spirit, for everything he said was true, and the fulfillment of what he tried to warn us about is at hand.

In the book he describes a snow bank not far from his home in the Alps:

The snow lies along that watershed, unbroken as a seeming unity. But when it melts, where it ends in its destination is literally thousands of miles apart. That is a watershed. That is what a watershed is. A watershed divides. A clear line can be drawn between what seems at first to be the same or at least very close, but in reality ends in different situations. A watershed is a line.[2]

He goes on to make what has proven to be a prophetic observation,

Evangelicals today are facing a watershed concerning the nature of biblical inspiration and authority…like the snow lying side by side on the ridge, the new views on biblical authority often seem at first glance not to be so very far from what evangelicals, until just recently, have always believed. But also, like the snow lying side by side on the ridge, the two views when followed consistently end up a thousand miles apart.[3]

Schaeffer points out that throughout most of the history of Christianity, inerrancy was a non-issue:

> There is a sense in which the problem of full biblical authority is fairly recent. Up until the last two hundred years or so, virtually every Christian believed in the complete inerrancy of the Bible, or in the equivalent of it expressed in similar terms. This was true both before the Reformation and after. The problem with the pre-Reformation church was not so much that it did not hold to the belief in an inerrant Bible as that it allowed the whole range of non-biblical theological ideas and superstitions to grow up within the church... note that the problem was not that the pre-Reformation church did not believe in the inerrancy of Scripture. The problem was that it did not practice the inerrancy of Scripture. It subordinated the Bible to its fallible teachings."[4]

How perfectly this describes what some are doing today, subordinating the Bible to fallible teachings. Today the inerrancy of the Bible is subordinated to the quest for cultural acceptance, and the talking points of the emergent Church are all about adapting to and even accommodating cultural practices which are clearly condemned in Scripture.

Well meaning, but wrong-headed ministers begin their preaching by stating that the church is irrelevant. This is usually followed by some sort of homage to notions like, "We are all on the same path'" and, "Who are we to say we are right and other religions are wrong?"

Schaeffer addresses this backwards thinking with these powerful remarks:

> Notice though what the primary problem was and is infiltration by a form of the world view which surrounds us, rather than the Bible being the unmovable base for judging the fallen culture... the Bible is bent to the culture..."[5]

As the Columbia River carves out gorges, radically changing the landscape, it "bends" the landscape. Without pushing the metaphor too far, I can say with no hesitation that the erosion of what used to be solid belief in a trust-worthy Bible has drastically changed the spiritual landscape as well and created dangerous waters in which to navigate. Sadly, many shipwrecks are testimony to the power of this momentum. Schaeffer predicted that what he was seeing in the late 1980s would, if unchecked, eventually morph into a dangerous syncretism which would ultimately contribute to laying the groundwork for devaluing of the sanctity of human life itself. Was he over-stating or exaggerating?

Let's look at the example he chose back in 1984, the whole abortion debate. When does life begin? Schaeffer cites an article that appeared in *Newsweek Magazine* January 11, 1982:

> The story of five or six pages showed conclusively that human life begins at conception. All students of biology should have known this all along. Then one turns the page and the next article is enti-tled, "But is it a person?" The conclusion of the page is, "The prob-lem is not determining when actual human life begins but when the value of that life begins to outweigh other considerations, such as the health, or even the happiness of the mother." The terrifying phrase is "…or even the happiness."[6]

In a mere thirty years we have gone from a speculative article bringing up a question in a *conversation* about whether or not a human being's life can be terminated because of the inconvenience it might cause to the mother to the present situation.

In 2014, legal protection is afforded by the federal government to doc-tors who perform so-called "late term abortions" complete with a demand that every taxpayer, including Christian institutions, pay for them.

As I considered that the Columbia is known for shipwrecks, I thought back to Paul's admonition to Timothy, "Some have made a shipwreck" (1 Tim. 1:19, KJV) of their faith. This is especially poignant language for him to have used. Paul, unlike any human being I have ever met, had undergone the ordeal of shipwreck, not once, but three times! (See 2 Cor. 11:2.)

He knew the horror of being swept up in seas that overwhelmed the ship. He knew what it was to face the jagged rocks as the surf pounded the ship to pieces. Thinking back to Schaeffer's watershed illustration, I thought how seemingly insignificant deviations from trust in the Bible can lead to just such dire circumstances. Embracing a belief concerning God's Word that is counter to God's revealed will is risky business.

I am thinking now of a young man who attended seminary with me. He was always questioning, always entertaining the latest speculation, trying to harmonize all the main religions of the world. He wasn't comfortable just accepting things. He ended up ultimately being asked to leave the seminary because he was caught proselytizing for a cult.

I told him not to mix with cult members who were pulling him away. He inferred that he had discernment and I needed to have an open mind. Shipwreck is the best word to describe what happened to him. He was a bright guy, a good man, but apparently he felt he was a little smarter than the rest of us reactionaries who refused to challenge the Bible.

When Tides and Currents Collide

I have had the privilege in my life not only to pastor for over thirty years, twenty of those years I also served as a Navy Reserve chaplain. Navy chaplains in their careers can expect to serve in Navy, Marine Corp, and Coast Guard units—all the sea services. While serving with the Coast Guard, I had the responsibility as the only reserve chaplain to the boat stations and the air stations on the Oregon Coast. I would train with the "Coasties" as they prepared to cross the bar to rescue a distressed mariner. I would fly with them as they trained to conduct search and rescue missions.

Once I was in the hangar of the air station sitting through a briefing on the possible problems to do with the Y2K panic. The alarm went off and all the air assets were immediately deployed. A supertanker had run aground and the crew needed to be airlifted off. This was a potential Exxon-Valdez moment. I was not allowed to fly with them on missions like this, so instead I went to the boat station at Winchester Bay.

"We're going to go out and escort a trawler across the bar, chaplain… want to come?"

My first inkling that this was going to be an interesting day was the fact that they equipped me with a survival suit and a helmet. *Now why would someone need a helmet on a boat?*

As we approached the bar (where the river meets the sea) the water was boiling with terrific turbulence. Hail began to fall and we began to sink into swells that reached twenty to thirty feet. A wall of green blocked out the horizon as we sank into the trough of these huge seas. I then understood why I needed a helmet and why I had been literally tethered to the boat. I felt that at any minute the boat would roll. I had been briefed on that very contingency. We were told how long to wait underwater before the boat would right itself.

I understood once again how powerful water can be, especially when tides and currents collide. After the ordeal was over, the coxswain decided not to waste this training opportunity. On the way back, when we were safely in the bay, they conducted a mock "man overboard" drill with the chaplain serving as the dummy.

As I bobbed in my relatively warm survival suit, I thought more than once about Paul and what he faced. These days I think about a whole generation of believers who are facing possible shipwreck because of what took place during a watershed debate about the inerrancy of the Bible.

Schaeffer observed:

Something has happened in the last sixty years. The freedom that once was founded on biblical consensus and a Christian ethos has now become *autonomous freedom, cut loose from all constraints.* (Emphasis mine.) Here we have the world spirit of our age-autonomous man setting himself up as God, in defiance of the knowledge and the moral truth which God has given.

His next remarks are a dire prophecy indeed.

When the memory of the Christian consensus which gave us freedom within the biblical form is increasingly forgotten, a manipulating authoritarianism will tend to fill the vacuum. An "elite," an authoritarianism as such, will gradually form on society so that it will not go into chaos—and most people would accept it.[7]

Humanism has a predictable trajectory—amorality followed by gross immorality. As morals dissipate and law is not enforced, lawlessness ensues, and Jesus Himself predicted that "because of the increase in lawlessness, the love of the many will wax cold" (Matt. 24:12, KJV). Abandoning inerrancy and insisting on cultural accommodation is, I believe, the natural result of *theological lawlessness* of a sort. The Bible as the source of propositional (ergo binding on everyone) truth is now being challenged at every turn. Someone goes to a Bible college or seminary. It soon becomes evident that the professors don't regard the Bible as the supernatural Word of God. Instead the unfortunate student is taught that the Bible is inspiring literature, just like other inspired literature, and just as open to literary criticism.

Disillusioned, many such students go on to experience a shipwreck of their faith. Perhaps they, like me, should have been issued a survival suit and a helmet.

As I read and re-read Schaeffer I was struck with how clearly he perceived the outcome we could expect once disbelief in an inerrant Bible would become entrenched. He predicted that human life itself would be devalued…and this would be facilitated by some measure of religious cover studiously prepared by academia.

Not that long ago I read a story in the *Eugene Register Guard* that literally stopped me in my tracks. The article described a grand opening ceremony of the new Planned Parenthood facility.[8] It was a dedication—if you will. (Dedication to what? To whom?)

There was a cleverly-crafted picture of a religious ceremony of sorts that accompanied the article. Some "clergy persons" decided to perform a rite in which they "christened the ground." Stop here and consider what happens in a so-called late-term abortion. Now try to use the word "christened" in the same sentence. As I read the disgusting account I thought of Francis Schaeffer and the alarm he sounded over thirty years ago.

Not that long ago I submitted an op-ed piece for consideration to the same newspaper. In it I showed what I believe to be the real back story of the Sandra Fluke case at Georgetown University. You may remember that this woman took on the leaders of the Catholic university, trying to force them to pay for her birth control (including the so-called morning-after pill). She became an instant celebrity and the progressive politicians used her as the poster girl for the narrative they crafted. It would become known as the "Republican war on women."[9] President Obama, notorious for voting "present" in lieu of taking controversial stands when he was a senator, was uncharacteristically definite in voting in support of partial-birth abortion. He called Ms. Fluke and personally apologized to her for her "mistreatment" at the hands of the Catholic Church. It came as no surprise to anyone paying attention when she was later invited to address the Democratic National Convention in September 2012, on the same day that same convention body ratified an official platform item defending federal funding for abortion on demand.

I wrote the op-ed to oppose the general tone of Catholic bashing and the misrepresenting of the real issue. I showed the clear linkage between the founder of Planned Parenthood, Margaret Sanger, and the eugenics movement that provided cover for the ethnic cleansing and Arian purification horrors of the Third Reich.[10]

The editor responsible for op-ed page initially didn't get back to me for quite a while. When I contacted him, he told me he had lost it, and that I should resubmit it. I did. Once again more time went by, further and further from the window of time of the actual Sandra Fluke incident; essentially allowing the issue to fade in the minds of the readers.

He then told me that he was going to print it but "just didn't feel right about it." He critiqued my line of thought and then suggested I would benefit from contacting the clergy person who christened the ground of the abortion clinic. Maybe this progressive pastor could help me get my thoughts straight?

If Francis Schaeffer's watershed analogy is valid, we can expect that time and distance would take the aberrant stream on a course that widens and widens and bends and turns changing the landscape as it builds momentum.

The same Democratic National Convention that had Sandra Fluke speak had what could best be described as a "telling" moment. The same platform that championed abortion rights had also omitted any mention of God—a first for either party.

The former Governor of Ohio, Ted Strickland, introduced an amendment to the platform wording which would include God. He began by touting his United Methodist ordination. He moved and the motion was seconded that the Convention should change the wording and insert verbiage that made mention of God in the platform. In the same discussion they also tried to clean up another mess.

They had inserted language that refused to acknowledge that Jerusalem was the capital of Israel. After the predictable outcry, and, I am sure, not a few focus groups and conference calls, they wanted to quickly show that the President really does acknowledge Jerusalem as the capital, and that God has a place in the platform.

The mayor of Los Angeles, serving in the role of convention chairman, was tasked with cleaning up this mess. He called for a two- thirds affirmation vote from the floor all in favor of amending the platform to include God and affirm Israel "All in favor say "Ay… Opposed? No."

What followed reflected the radical changes that have taken place in our culture due in no small part to the abandonment of God's Word. The majority of the delegates screamed "No!" (They doubled down on their position that they wanted to leave the very mention of God out of their deliberations and that they do not affirm that Jerusalem is Israel's capital).

At the same convention, the first lady received rave reviews for her speech in which she linked the rights of same-sex couples to wed with the civil rights struggle of Martin Luther King Jr. (hence inferring moral equivalency). Think of it, an entire political movement taking public stands against the revealed will of God as it is found in the Bible.

Where were the pastors? Where was the outcry? Francis Schaeffer was right when he observed:

> Despite claims of cultural relevance, an accommodating evangelicalism also leaves the surrounding culture increasingly unchanged.[11]

I would add that the culture does, however, leave the church greatly changed…and that not for the good.

Schaeffer rightly concludes that the attempt to "fit" in this increasingly godless culture is the reason behind the intentional vagueness concerning biblical inerrancy:

> The central theme of contemporary theology is accommodation to modernity. It is the underlying motif that unites the seemingly vast differences between existential theology, process theology, liberation theology, demythologization, and many varieties of liberal theology—all *searching for some more compatible adjustment to modernity.*"[12] (Emphasis mine.)

Is not this desperate attempt to "fit in" with an increasingly pagan culture eerily similar to the Nicolaitin compromise described in The Book of The Revelation? The Nicolaitins were apparently committed to a posture of compromise with the pagan culture. Don't rock the boat, blend in, don't confront.

Paul in his letters had to address this issue of accommodation over and over. The epistles of Second Peter and Jude dealt exclusively with this whole issue of compromise and accommodation. I can honestly say that every person I have met who has embraced the emergent notion that "there is no such thing as propositional truth" also exhibits great discomfort with what they deem problematic references in the Bible that are explicitly counter to the postmodern culture in which we live.

Emergent leader Brian McClaren declared a moratorium against even discussing gender issues. I wonder how many people know about this "detail" that may have influenced his "theology."

Brian McLaren caused quite a stir in 2010 when he announced in his book *A New Kind of Christianity* that he no longer believes that homosexuality is a sin. Many people were surprised by the news simply because he himself had called on evangelicals in 2006 to observe a five-year moratorium on making moral pronouncements about homosexuality…yet in the book, McLaren not only made a moral pronouncement, he also chastised conservative evangelicals for their views on the matter.

At the time, it appeared that McLaren's revisionist views were merely a part of his emerging theological outlook—a postmodern slouch toward theological liberalism. No doubt it was that, as his writings make perfectly clear. But could there have been more to it than that?

The *New York Times* reported that McLaren had recently presided over his own son's same-sex commitment ceremony. This would seem to imply that from the time McLaren called a "moratorium" to the time that he wrote *A New Kind of Christianity*, he was dealing with the issue not merely as a detached observer but as one with a deeply personal stake in the matter. I don't pretend to account for all of the influences over McLaren's thinking, but it's hard to imagine that his son's situation would not have had some sort of an impact on McLaren's theological revisions.

If that is the case, I think there are many Christians who could immediately relate to his circumstance. It is very difficult when one has a close friend or family member who is gay and who differs with what the Bible teaches about sexual norms.

> There is an incredible cultural pressure for the Christian to break the relational impasse by revising Christianity's teaching on human sexuality. No one wants to alienate loved ones. Also, no one wants to be labeled a bigot. The desire to avoid pariah status is why many people are simply moving away from a traditional view of marriage. People do not want to offend their gay friends, neighbors, and family members."[13]

This reticence, this balking at forthrightly declaring all the Word of God, including verses that offend people, is, I believe, the result of the erosion of the banks of orthodoxy caused by the flood of debris, and the confluence with "other rivers" that comprises the emergent "conversation."

Back to the Coast Guard for a moment. I am in awe of these young men and women. They, even more than the other sea services, often place very junior people in command positions.

The people who drive the boats are called coxswains. The people who are going to be tasked with actually going into the surf to rescue people are held to an even higher standard. Their rating is called "Surf-man." They train at one of the most dangerous places on earth, a place described as one of the most hazardous river bars in the world.

It is called Cape Disappointment. It is located right where the mighty Columbia River meets the sea. This is the place where so many shipwrecks have taken place that these highly trained professionals have plenty of opportunity to learn their craft. They must learn to trust their vessel and their crew, and, most of all, their training. The majority of that training is the result of lessons learned by others who didn't fare so well in these stormy seas. Will we learn from the shipwrecks of those who have drifted from trust in an inerrant Bible, or will we carelessly plunge into the frothy seas trusting only in our own wits and opinions?

I have been fascinated as I traced the Columbia from its tiny watershed all the way to Cape Disappointment. In some ways, my life and ministry have followed the course of that river. It was in Salmon Arm British Columbia near the headwaters of the Columbia that I first heard about The New Age Movement.

Years later I moved back to the United States and pastored in Oregon for over twenty years. I now reside about an hour away from where the Columbia winds its way through a magical place which the Independent Film Channel has dubbed "Portlandia."

Portland is home to emergent notables, William Paul Young, the author of *The Shack*, Dan Merchant of *Lord Save Us From Your Followers* fame, and Donald Miller, author of *Blue Like Jazz*. Emergent seminary professor Leonard Sweet also calls the Rose City home.

I will have more to say about these individuals later on, but I think for now it is safe to say that Francis Schaeffer was right. Deviation from orthodoxy regarding the inerrancy of Scripture seems at first to be a miniscule, almost trivial thing. Given a long enough period of time—in this instance only thirty years—one can see how rapidly erosion due to such deviation can lead to apostasy and shipwreck.

> A river reaches places which its source never knows.
>
> OSWALD CHAMBERS

It was in 1990, in that place not far from the headwaters of the Columbia, that I first encountered the New Age Movement attempting to blend progressive politics with New Age spirituality. When I wrote against it then, I had no idea how far things would have progressed in a relatively short period of time. What started as a creek took a direction and merged with other rivers and took a bend and another bend and wound its way through a path that has and will, I believe, ultimately lead to shipwrecks.

Dr. David Jeremiah has written a powerful book with a provocative title, *I Never Thought I'd See the Day.* I can relate. I never thought I'd see the day when someone like emergent author Rob Bell would even have a hearing let alone be invited to address what used to be mainline conservative denominations.

I never thought I'd see the day when members of *The Jesus Seminar* would be quoted as credible sources by ministers serving in denominations whose statements of faith affirm the inerrancy of the Bible.

I never thought I'd see the day when someone dressed up like a minister would "christen the ground" of an abortion facility, or when the President of the United States would openly affirm that he supports partial-birth abortion and gay marriage. Things are moving at breakneck speed.

There exists for the first time in my lifetime the very real possibility that preaching the Bible may land you in jail in the United States. Current conversations about hate speech may in fact find their way into the law books. In Europe and in Canada this is already the case.

Francis Schaeffer concluded his book with this observation:

> As we have now come to the famed year 1984, what we need in light of the accommodation around us is a generation of radicals for truth and for Christ. We need a young generation and others who will be willing to stand for loving confrontation, but real confrontation, with the current forms of the world spirit as they surround us today, and in contrast to the way in which so much of evangelicalism has developed the autonomic mentality to each successive point.[14]

One cannot only survive Cape Disappointment, it is possible to also pluck the victims of shipwreck out of the seas which threaten to kill them. But you had better be ready. The Motto of The US Coast Guard is *Semper Paratus* which means "Always Prepared."

Paul exhorted Timothy, "Be prepared in season and out of season" (2 Tim. 4:2). Another verse says, "Always be prepared to give an account for the hope that is within you" (1 Pet. 3:15, KJV).

A word of caution though, being prepared and actually launching into the storm are two entirely different things. Being personally prepared is crucial, but the vessel that carries you better be watertight. The *unofficial* motto of the Coast Guard rescue crews is "You have to go out—you don't have to come back," which alludes to the inherent danger in our search and rescue mission.

The gospel which we preach as "the power of God unto salvation" comes from what used to be universally deemed to be an inerrant Bible. We have a mission, a rescue mission in the truest sense of those words. Like the scared chaplain tethered to the hull with his helmet on, we need not fear shipwreck, and we can save those "in peril on the sea." But the trustworthiness of the vessel matters.

It matters a lot.

THREE

WHERE'S THE RUNAWAY LANE?

It was never my purpose in this book to reargue the debate as to whether the Scriptures are inerrant. I do believe, though, that it is helpful to summarize some key battles that have taken place in the fairly recent past that have to do with the importance of the issue. I want to show how others have framed this debate, and why it matters, or should matter to us today.

Charles Haddon Spurgeon has been called "The Prince of Preachers." He remains one of the most quoted ministers of all time, and his books grace the libraries of many seminaries and pastors' studies. In the last years of his life, he became embroiled in what he labeled "The Great Down Grade Controversy." In short, he dared to confront his fellow pastors and professors, and more to the point, the Baptist Union he himself helped found, that had embraced the so called "Higher Criticism" of the Bible.

Spurgeon's imagery of a downgrade is very familiar to me in that I lived for a number of years in the interior of British Columbia, and often drove in the mountains. As one approaches the summit, signs begin to appear warning that soon you will be descending, and the road will take on a steep grade…a downgrade.

You are cautioned to pull over and check your brakes. You are also warned to recognize that momentum may cause great danger. This is especially important for big rigs, in that once they start down that grade they are committed to a course that may soon take on a life of its own. It was never very comforting to me to smell burnt clutch, or overheated brakes just in time to see a logging truck in my rearview mirror. *Nothing good can come of this*, I thought.

Spurgeon's position was that once the Bible was devalued, and scholars treated it just like any other literature, a dangerous breach would occur that would ultimately have disastrous and unintended consequences, but disastrous nonetheless. He attempted to call the Baptist Union back to its own doctrinal position. The battle was so vicious and became so personal that later his widow would say without hesitation that the controversy contributed to Spurgeon's early death.

Dennis M. Swanson has given us a helpful summary of what happened as a result of the controversy. In his paper, "The Great Down Grade Controversy and Evangelical Boundaries: Some Lessons from Spurgeon's Battle for the Bible," he cites six areas of variance from orthodoxy that resulted from modern evangelicals questioning (as they did in Spurgeon's day) truths that used to be held as the standard that defined what it meant to be an evangelical:

The very nature of God, abandoning a theistic view for more of a "process model" of God.

Challenging traditional Christology and emphasizing a position that portrays a lower view, stressing not Jesus' divinity, but His humanity.

The substitutionary atonement is challenged and a change of emphasis takes place to a more universalist tone.

The long-held belief that the Bible was inerrant in all of its claims is replaced with verbiage that infers that the Bible is largely infallible i.e. In areas that lead us to Christ it is without error, but that is not necessarily so in areas of science or history.

Direct creation is now to be replaced with theistic evolution.

And finally, traditional hermeneutics are replaced with post-modern theories. No one can know to any truly meaningful extent the author's original intent.[1] (My paraphrase and summary of Swanson's remarks.)

This would be, as one writer put it, "one of those conflicts which reappear in history when opposing ideas can no longer refuse battle."

I thought, as I read this thorough treatment of the effects of The Down Grade Controversy, of a description of what has become known in our day (at least for the next few months as these things morph regularly) as *Open Source Theology*.

Andrew Perriman gives the rationale for a new theology to address Emergent Church needs:

> I started Open Source theology out of the conviction that if there is such a thing as Emerging Church (I think there is but I'm less sure what it is) and if it is, deep down, a work of God (I think it is) then it urgently needs an emerging theology. It seems to me that we are wasting our time if we rethink church without at the same time rethinking the story that gives church a reason for existing at all.

Note his language here, it is the *story*, not the Bible or worse— not God or Jesus—the *story* gives the church its reason for existence. He adds,

> Traditionally, theology has been generated by experts, marketed and retailed by pastors and teachers and passively consumed by church goers. [Do you hear the condescension in his remarks?] That sort of approach, for all its strengths, sits uncomfortably with the ethos of the Emerging Church. The Open Source paradigm offers an alternative method. An open source theology is the product of a public conversation by all those who have a serious interest in the subject; it is responsive to the user environment; it is exploratory, open minded, incomplete, less concerned to establish fixed points and boundaries than to nurture a thoughtful and constructive dialogue between text and context.[2]

"Open source" is computer language. It is collaborative. It is the product of "group think." One reason that many universities will not allow citations from Wikipedia from their students is the fact that Wikipedia is also open source. People can, on their own initiative, change what appears to be encyclopedic references on any topic. Everyone's input is given equal weight.

What Spurgeon recognized and confronted in the Great Down Grade Controversy is captured in this statement that appeared in *The Sword and the Trowell:*

> The present struggle is not a debate upon the question of Calvinism or Arminianism, but of the truth of God versus the inventions of men. All who believe in the gospel should unite against that "modern thought" which is its deadly enemy… A new religion has been initiated, which is no more Christianity than chalk is cheese, and this religion is destitute of moral honesty, palms itself off as the old faith with slight improvements, and on this plea usurps pulpits which were erected for gospel preaching. The Atonement is scuttled, the inspiration of Scripture is derided, the Holy Spirit is degraded into an influence, the punishment of sin is turned into fiction and the resurrection into a myth.[3]

Spurgeon's last address to his pastors college conference was titled "The Greatest Fight in the World." This last call to theological orthodoxy was delivered just six months before his death.

Dennis Swanson gives us a warning worth heeding:

> Beyond these disturbing theological trends, the key lesson to be learned from the Down-Grade Controversy is the need for diligence. Spurgeon himself warned, "There is truth and there is error and these are opposite the one to the other. Do not indulge yourselves in the folly with which so many are duped… that truth may be error, an error may be truth, that black is white and white is black, and there is a whitey-brown that goes between, which perhaps is best of the whole lot."[4]

John MacArthur, in an address to graduating students about to embark on their ministries preached a message entitled, "Ministry in an Age of Itching Ears." He spoke of the Great Down Grade Controversy and then observed,

> Here we are a hundred years later and history is again repeating itself. The church again has become worldly, and not just worldly but studiously so…winds of doctrinal compromise are beginning to stir. False doctrine and worldliness, the two things Spurgeon warned about, the very two influences he attacked always go hand in hand. And listen to this, worldliness usually leads the way.

In the same address MacArthur cites a leading author who wrote:

> I believe that developing a marketing orientation is precisely what the church needs to do if we are to make a difference in the spiritual health of this nation for the remainder of this century. My contention based on careful study of data and the activities of churches is that the major problem plaguing the church is its failure to embrace a marketing orientation in what has become a market driven environment.[5]

The implications of this are obvious, says MacArthur.

> *Marketing principles are becoming the arbiter of truth.* [Emphasis added.] Elements of the message that don't fit the promotional plan are simply omitted. Marketing savvy demands that the offence of the cross must be downplayed. Salesmanship requires that the negative subjects like divine wrath must be avoided. Consumer satisfaction means that the standard of righteousness cannot be raised too high.[6]

After a recent district convention of one denomination, a questionnaire (survey monkey) was sent out asking the pastors to "critique their worship experience." What kind of experience would they prefer? What songs do they like? The choice of which speakers and worship leaders would be invited to minister at the next convention would be based on the results of this survey.

Being aware of what people like is one thing. Pandering like this though is nothing less than the capitulation to the World Spirit of autonomous freedom that Schaeffer warned us about. I thought of a remark made by Lady Margaret Thatcher. She said, "Consensus is the abdication of leadership."

MacArthur illustrates what this menu driven mentality must inevitably yield:

In periods of unsettled faith, says one writer, and skepticism in matters of religion, teachers of all kinds swarm like the flies in Egypt and the demand creates the supply. The hearers invite and shape their own preachers. If people desire a calf to worship, a ministerial calf maker is readily found.[7]

Not in all of my life have I ever prepared an address as minutely and meticulously as I have this one. I have been a pastor for fifty-eight years.

These sobering remarks were contained in a message preached by Dr. W.A. Criswell to The Southern Baptists Pastors Conference held in Dallas, Texas, in June of 1985. His outline consisted of the following points:

- The Pattern of death for a denomination
- The Pattern of death of an Institution
- The Pattern of death for a Preacher, a Professor, and finally,
- The Promise of Renascence, the Resurrection and Revival.

Criswell warned the Baptists about the concessions that were taking place concerning inerrancy. Citing Spurgeon biographer, Dr. Arnold Dallimore, Criswell wrote,

Where there is no acceptance of the Bible as inerrant, there is no true Christianity. The preaching is powerless, and what Spurgeon declared to his generation a hundred years ago is the outcome.[8]

He told a story which illustrates the dilemma faced by pastors who don't believe the Bible is inerrant:

A friend of mine went to the University of Chicago to gain a PhD in pedagogy. While there he made the friendship of a student in the Divinity school. This budding preacher said to my teacher friend, "I am in a great quandary. I have been called to the pastorate of a Presbyterian church in the Midwest, but it is one of those old fashioned Presbyterian Churches that believes the Bible, and I do not believe the Bible, and I don't know what to do." My teacher friend replied "I can tell you exactly what you ought to do… I think that if you don't believe the Bible, you ought to quit the ministry."

Criswell's sense of urgency is evident in these remarks:

Our own and our ultimate destiny lies in the offing. Seemingly we stand at the continental divide of history and the very watershed of civilization. Changes of colossal nature are sweeping the world.[9]

A writer from another era, C.H. Mackintosh, voiced similar concerns. He begins by quoting someone who was advocating for a more liberal approach to interpreting Scripture who said, "We must present truth in such an aspect as will attract."

Mackintosh countered,

What is really meant is this, that truth is to be made a kind of variable, elastic thing, which can be turned into any shape, or stretched to any length, to suit the tastes of those who would desire to put it out of the world altogether. Truth, however, cannot be thus treated; it can never be made to reduce itself to the level of this world. It will speak distinctly if its voice be not stifled.

The attempt to accommodate truth to those who are of the world can only end in complete failure. There can be no accommodation. Let it stand upon its own heavenly height; let saints stand fully and firmly with it; let us invite sinners up to it; but let us not descend to the low and groveling pursuits of the world, and thus rob truth, so far as in us lies, of all its edge and power.

We may think to commend truth to the minds of worldly people by an effort to conform to their ways; but so far from commending it, we in reality expose it to secret contempt and scorn. The man who conforms to the world will be an enemy of Christ and an enemy of the people of God. It cannot be otherwise.[10]

Mackintosh rightly shows that once accommodation begins, truth loses its essence…its fixed, unchangeable nature. The Down Grade that Spurgeon described has resulted in catastrophic events. The only hope now is the use of runaway lanes. These are steep *upgraded* roads often made of sand. In a last ditch attempt to save his load and his life, a trucker can find a runaway lane and hope the steep grade in the upward slanted direction will slow the momentum and safely bring his rig to a stop.

Extreme conditions call for extreme countermeasures. Much of what I have to say in this book may seem too confrontational and unduly blunt. I am willing to be misunderstood. For years I stood by knowing "someone" should say something.

Our pastors' conferences used to be events highlighted by passionate calls to repentance and altar services with ministers on their knees crying out to God for the power of the Holy Spirit to fall afresh. Now, some ministers tweet their thoughts to each other during the meeting as they weigh the latest poll results being presented by experts in culture. We're careening down a steep grade, and apparently, our brakes are failing.

Which road we choose has life and death implications. In a poem by Robert Frost these lines have always given me pause for reflection.

The Road Not Taken

Two roads diverged in a yellow wood,

And sorry I could not travel both

And be one traveler, long I stood

And looked down one as far as I could

To where it bent in the undergrowth;

Then took the other, as just as fair,

And having perhaps the better claim,

Because it was grassy and wanted wear;

Though as for that the passing there

Had worn them really about the same,

And both that morning equally lay

In leaves no step had trodden black.

Oh, I kept the first for another day!

Yet knowing how way leads on to way,

I doubted if I should ever come back.

I shall be telling this with a sigh

Somewhere ages and ages hence:

Two roads diverged in a wood, and I— I took the one less traveled by,

And that has made all the difference.[11]

I can envision a time in the not too distant future when seminaries will simply become absorbed into universities, and the study of theology will morph into a hodgepodge of the study of literature, cultural diversity, and various and sundry gender and race studies. Comparative religions classes will replace theology altogether and Church history will be taught by revisionists pushing a one-world spirituality.

People like Spurgeon, Criswell, MacArthur, and Schaeffer have sounded an alarm. Does that matter to you? For the sake of the generations to come it should. Perhaps it's time to pull over, stop, and check our brakes.

FOUR

ABOUT BRIDGES

The generation of those who first give up biblical inerrancy may have a warm evangelical background and real personal relationship with Jesus Christ so that they can live theologically on the basis of their limited-inerrancy viewpoint. But what happens when the next generation tries to build on that foundation? I am saying that whether it takes five or fifty years, any denomination or para-church group that forsakes inerrancy will end up shipwrecked. It is impossible to prevent the surrender of other important doctrinal teachings of the Word of God when inerrancy is gone.

FRANCIS SCHAEFFER

When I attended Fuller Seminary in the eighties, I was introduced to the writings of Dr. Donald McGavran, who some have called "The Father of Modern Missions." Dr. McGavran wrote on the subject *The Bridges of God*. His theories changed the perceptions of an entire generation of church leaders. He asked,

The question is how, in a manner true to the Bible, can a Christian movement be established in some class, caste, tribe or other segment of society which will, over a period of years, so bring groups of its related families to Christian faith that the whole people is Christianized?[1]

His phrase "the bridges of God" describes linkages that already exist. Natural affinity exists between extended family and clans. He used the term *homogeneous units* to describe these groups or tribes or "hidden people groups."

We should, he wrote, recognize that these bridges already exist and adapt our mission strategy to reaching the entire people group. His use of the term a "Christian Movement" caught my attention. There certainly is wisdom in recognizing the ethos of the community in which we serve. There is also a lot to be said for being intentional and disciplined in thinking about how to engage people. Are we, though, tasked with forming a "movement" or reaching individuals one by one? It's an important distinction.

Clearly McGavran's insight was revolutionary. I believe that what some Church Growth experts have developed based on McGavran's "homogeneous unit principle," however, has taken on a new meaning, something much more secular. Modern marketing techniques entered the equation, and now there is a heavy reliance upon polls, surveys, and demographic studies.

Paul Smith, author of *New Evangelicalism: The New World Order* makes the following observation about developments at Fuller Seminary:

All these issues led to a broader definition of evangelicalism, which morphed into what became more commonly known as "new evangelicalism." Now there was a new movement; it was self-defined as Christian, but it fully endorsed inclusiveness and accommodation because it opened the door to many who no longer believed in the inerrancy of the Bible. Sadly, deception and full lack of candor were involved.[2]

Smith, in another passage of his book reminded his readers that Francis Schaeffer predicted inerrancy was the watershed issue that would determine the future of evangelicalism,

Errancy and inerrancy of Scripture constitute two mutually exclusive principles. A choice once made will determine where one ends up. Shaeffer said it so well. 'The generation of those who first give up biblical inerrancy may have a warm evangelical background and real personal relationship with Jesus Christ so that they can live theologically on the basis of their limited-inerrancy viewpoint. But what happens when the next generation tries to build on that foundation? *I am saying that whether it takes five or fifty years, any denom-*

ination or parachurch group that forsakes inerrancy will end up ship-wrecked. [Emphasis mine.] It is impossible to prevent the surrender of other important doctrinal teachings of the Word of God when inerrancy is gone.[3]

Paul Smith shows what developed over time at Fuller:

As Fuller Seminary continued its drift, it increasingly became the nurturing place of the postmodern Church growth and Emerging Movements. World mission became missiology. The School of World Mission became The School of Intercultural Studies. The new paradigm morphed from World Mission (singular) to the studies (plural) of culture, anthropology, sociology and psychology; with the objective of becoming postmodern and seeker friendly in order to better communicate with the postmodern homogeneous groups. Accommodation became the oil that lubricated the process.[4]

To refer to a person as an "ologist" is to infer that he or she is an "expert" by virtue of a certain level of mastery of a technique or a science. Bartenders for instance, are now "mixologists."

The Church Growth experts took McGavran's principle and expanded upon it to such a degree that now, much more attention is paid to describing and distinguishing these special homogeneous units than there is to preserving the integrity and clarity of the gospel we are preaching.

The emphasis has changed. Once upon a time the consensus was that the starting point of any outreach was the proclamation of the Gospel; which was solely based on the Word of God. The task at hand was getting the Word out.

Now it seems that the starting point is a demographic study of the felt needs or perceived needs of the "target audience." The primary task one hears about today is that of demonstrating to the culture that we do not present a threat. If this involves affirming practices that are overtly forbidden in the Word, then we will just not talk about those things. We will, instead, stress the general topics of love and justice, avoiding specific scriptural directives that speak to the most destructive behaviors rife in the current culture.

In America the application of these principles looks like this. An individual senses a call to reach a certain group or a certain area with the gospel. Sometimes the location of the church plant (already an old-fashioned term) is decided upon based largely on the preference of the leader of the team.

I heard of one young man who worked out a plan to take a team to start a "missional community" in Seattle. When asked why he chose Seattle…he knew no one there nor had he himself ever been there… he said he picked Seattle because "that was where the Twilight movies were filmed and he liked the vibe of the place."

Think with me for a minute. He picked the place because of a blockbuster movie about vampires which hit a nerve (or a vein) with a generation of young people obsessed with the occult. Giving him the benefit of the doubt, I assume that his decision was based on what he perceived to be some sort of affirmation of the pop culture. Wanting to accommodate, he then apparently crafted his plan.

Is there anything inherently wrong with thinking about evangelism this way? I don't presume to know what was in this man's heart. I never met him. I do remember, though, that on more than one occasion the Apostle Paul made plans on his own initiative to go to this place or that place only to be prevented by the Holy Spirit. The places where the Lord sent him often erupted in riots as a result of the message he brought… not the predictable response to a seeker-sensitive initiative.

At one time I had a whole shelf of books in my library on Church Growth strategies. I must have attended over a dozen conferences over the years. Here is some of what I learned about the process of planning to reach a community and start a church.

Once the site is identified, then marketing plans and demographics studies take place. Ministry is executed as much more of a business plan, constantly revised and critiqued. The team is obsessed with numbers and statistics. I remember hearing at Fuller that the only way this current generation would be reached would be for the church to adopt modern advertising strategies and marketing plans.

I once read a Church planting proposal from a fellow doctor of ministry student. He described his "target audience" and his plan to reach them. Listen to how he described his future parishioners:

- They would be white. (He actually said that.)
- They would be between 27 and 35 years of age.
- They would have a mean net income of between $45,000 and $60,000.
- He cited a list of FM stations they would prefer.
- He listed the types of bistros and cafes they would frequent.
- He described the cars they would drive and the clothes they would wear.
- He then submitted his plan for a grade.

How important is the start point? Do we have permission to just decide on our own initiative to begin a bridge to a community or group based on our feelings or our accommodation to the culture? Are there any consequences to failing to heed the Bible before we plan anything? The next chapter shows what can happen if we "eyeball it."

FIVE

"YOU EYEBALLED IT, DIDN'T YOU?"

As I mentioned earlier, part of my Reserve Chaplain Career involved serving with the Marines. In that capacity while serving with a company of combat engineers which was tasked with building bridges, I learned a lesson I will never forget.

It was raining. It seemed like every drill weekend it was raining. This particular weekend we were camped out in a rock quarry along the river. Our assignment was to build a certain type of bridge to cross the river.

I had previously seen pallets of pre-engineered steel components stored at the Reserve Center. I noted at the time that I didn't see cranes or other heavy equipment to the degree I might have expected. This weekend, I would learn why.

This particular type of bridge was designed to be assembled in pieces like a giant erector set, and it was designed to be assembled by manpower. Those pallets of bridge components also contained lifting bars. Two Marines or four Marines or how many as were needed would put on their gloves, pick up their lifting bars, and literally lift each piece into position for assembly. It was backbreaking work…and did I mention it was raining?

A little background here might be instructive. The command structure of a Marine Reserve unit is comprised of both active duty and reserve components. Active duty Marines serve as instructors and facilitators and the reserve unit with its own commanding officer learns the skills necessary to function in a combat environment. The senior officer of the active duty component is known as the Inspector/Instructor or "I and I" for short.

On this weekend, the Inspector/Instructor stood by relatively passively as the reserve officer took command and gave orders to begin the bridge building. This particular type of bridge is assembled on one river bank *by hand*. It was raining; did I mention that?

Once the bridge superstructure was completed on one bank of the river, a boom component would be thrust across to the other side where the rest of the construction would take place. Once complete, the bridge would be sturdy enough to handle both people and vehicle traffic.

My job as chaplain was to be with the troops as they accomplished this arduous task, encouraging them, ripping open an MRE and sharing coffee with them on their break, being the comic relief as I attempted to do even a portion of the hard labor… all the while affirming them.

It really was inspiring to watch these young devil dogs as they strained to lift each piece of solid steel, and then bolt each plate piece in place. All day long as the rain came down, they counted and lifted in unison…piece by piece…knuckle busting…dirty…sandy…grubby hard work.

At the end of what seemed like three days instead of one, the pieces were all assembled. The commander gave the order, and the exhausted Marines prepared for one last herculean effort to thrust the boom across the river. "ONE…TWO…THREE"…and they pushed with all their might… nothing.

Two…three times more…they redoubled their efforts… "PUSH!"… nothing. The officer in charge began to sweat. Finally the order came to "stand by" and the Inspector/Instructor and the commander took a little walk.

I was close enough to overhear their conversation. To his credit, the active duty officer didn't berate the officer in charge. As they looked off in the opposite direction together I overheard the Inspector Instructor say, "You eyeballed it, didn't you?"

Despite protestations to the contrary, the officer in charge admitted that perhaps at the very beginning of the exercise he may have just estimated or "eyeballed it," but the rest of the day, he consulted the book.

"You should have started by the book at the very beginning. All you did was add tons of weight to something that wasn't in alignment from the start. You'll have to do it all over."

And so the Marines used every colorful word in their lexicon, grabbed some MRE's, and then put their gloves back on (oh, and did I say it was raining?), took the whole thing apart bit by bit…piece by piece…and then started it all over again. Only this time it was by the book, from step one to the finish.

The Inspector/Instructor taught a powerful lesson. The officer in charge learned a powerful lesson, and a soggy chaplain learned perhaps the most powerful lesson of all. For you see the whole time I heard those two officers talking, I thought about the authority of the Bible, and the absolute necessity of living "by the Book."

I was witnessing a parable. In preparing to write this book, I thought back to this rainy bridge day bridge-building exercise. As church leaders, we can be well intentioned in our efforts to build a bridge to reach people for the Lord. We can exert incredible amounts of energy. We can even motivate others to redouble their efforts. We can have team building exercises—*esprit d' corps*— if you will.

At the end of the day, however, if what we do, we attempt to do in our strength, we'll end up doing what seems best to us (eyeballing it) rather than consulting our manual—the Bible. Our best bridge may look nice, but can't help people safely reach the other side.

All the weighty improvisations, clever though they be, will not account for failing to consult the Book from the outset. Anything built on a less than God's specified start point will eventually be immobilized by its own weight. Hence the purpose in writing this book.

Throughout my entire ministry, I have been watching and warning and preaching because *I see something*. There has been a steady, methodical relentless assault on the authority of the Scriptures. The notion of an inerrant Bible and the very idea of such a thing as propositional truth are now looked upon as relics from an irrelevant past—ideas destined for the dust bin of history.

Emergent church writer Phyllis Tickle has actually said that every five hundred years or so the church needs to have a *rummage sale* (the inference being, "to throw out useless stuff" that no one wants anymore). What is shocking to me is that she was referring to the doctrines of the Protestant Reformation, and the main doctrine known as *Sola Scriptura*... Only the Scriptures.[1]

We are obsessed with innovation. We hold conference after conference on how to build bridges to people. We write books and read books on "how to be relevant." Think about that for a minute… *The Church of the living God needing to consult ad men and social scientists in order to accommodate the world spirit…to be perceived as relevant…?*

I remember an incident that took place when George W. Bush was president. The press hounded him relentlessly, always probing, looking to trap him in a "gotcha" moment.

One clever reporter cited a critic who inferred that the President was no longer *relevant*. President Bush took the bait and said, "I'm relevant." Well guess what the press did with that sound bite? For months they played it over and over again. He had been tricked into giving weight to a question that was designed to put him on the defensive, and by answering he gave credibility to the assumption… a contrived assumption of his perceived irrelevance.

I believe that denominations, seminaries, and Christians in general have fallen prey to a similar ploy. Emergent church writers say the same thing again and again in one form or another. "In this postmodern era, none of the old ideas will work in reaching this generation."

Once this premise is uttered, Christian pollsters oblige with survey after survey confirming the conventional wisdom that the church must totally revamp its methods and sadly *alter its message* to reach these special people who would never respond to something as "old school" as altar calls and preaching the certainty of Jesus Christ as the only savior.

What does *postmodern* mean anyway? I came across this insightful description of the term:

A general and wide-ranging term which is applied to literature, art, philosophy, architecture, fiction, and cultural and literary criticism, among others. Postmodernism is largely a reaction to the assumed certainty of scientific, or objective, efforts to explain reality. In essence, it stems from a recognition that reality is not simply mirrored in human understanding of it, but rather, is constructed as the mind tries to understand its own particular and personal reality.

For this reason, postmodernism is highly skeptical of explanations which claim to be valid for all groups, cultures, traditions, or races, and instead focuses on the relative truths of each person. In the postmodern understanding, interpretation is everything; reality only comes into being through our interpretations of what the world means to us individually. Postmodernism relies on concrete experience over abstract principles, knowing always that the outcome of one's own experience will necessarily be fallible and relative, rather than certain and universal.[2]

From that definition I glean that postmodernism is:

- Primarily a reaction
- That it constructs reality in the mind rather than relying on objective truth
- That reality only "comes into being" in our interpretation
- That personal experience trumps objective propositional truth.

Thinking about the implications of this for bridge building, I try to imagine a bridge being built based on these criteria. What would a bridge be like if it was built solely based on a reactionary approach which emphasized interpretation and downplayed proposition truths like the laws of physics?

One of the signs of a community in decline is a crumbling infrastructure. In the recent federal government stimulus package, which was supposed to kick start the economy, one of the first areas of investment was to be the repair of unsafe bridges. What makes for a safe, reliable bridge? For a bridge to be safe, it must be the product of both engineered plans and tested materials. And once built, bridges need to be inspected and maintained. Let's look at each of these criteria.

A BRIDGE MUST BE DESIGNED AND ENGINEERED ACCORDING TO PRECISE SPECIFICATION.

Engineers' plans are the result of years of study of the laws of physics and metallurgy and other sciences. They also, I hazard a guess, are the product of "lessons learned" from bridges that have failed. Back to the Marine bridge builders. Long before we crawled back onto our shelter halves the night of that bridge building exercise, the Marines met to have a "lessons learned" debriefing. What happened? What did we learn? How could we ensure that this mistake wasn't repeated?

Throughout Church History there have been attempts to bridge the gap between the Gospel and the world by accommodation to the pagan culture. One group of believers referred to in the Book of The Revelation, the Nicolaitins, decided that the way to build a successful bridge to the pagans around them was by participating in the same abominable practices of those around them—practices which Jesus said He hates. Strong language. One might take pause here, Jesus said He *hates* this.

One commentator describes this group as:

A Christian group within the churches of Asia Minor whose professed insight into the divine allowed them freedom to become part of their syncretistic pagan society.[3]

Professor Mounce, (author of a great commentary on *The Revelation*), points out that this participation in pagan rites was not only an act of compromise, it was also a rebellious act in that the Nicolaitins violated the Apostles' doctrine found in Acts 15. The Gentiles joining the church were "to refrain from food sacrificed to idols and sexual immorality."[4]

No matter the particulars of the Nicolaitin heresy, the Lord is clear that He is commending the Ephesians for rejecting it and hating this accommodation to pagan culture just as He does. In the message to the Church at Pergamum (Rev. 2), the Lord points out that some are holding to the teaching of Balaam. Balaam, you may remember, had advised the Midianite women how to beguile the Israelites into acting treacherously against the Lord (Num. 25).

One commentator wrote that Balaam's clever notion was to break down Israel's power by an indirect attack on their morale.

Pagan food and Pagan women were his powerful tools against the rigidity of the Mosaic laws…thus *Balaam became a prototype of all corrupt teachers who betrayed believers into fatal compromise with worldly ideologies.* [Emphasis mine.] At Pergamum accommodation was the wisest policy.[5]

One final illustration found in *The Revelation* is the warning to the church at Thyatira:

The Thyatiran Jezebel is probably some prominent woman within the church, who, like her Old Testament counterpart, was influencing the people of God to forsake loyalty to God by promoting a tolerance toward and involvement in pagan practices. This extended to fornication and participation in the religious feasts connected with membership in the trade guilds.[6]

Mounce makes a powerful observation about the teaching of this Jezebel:

It is questionable whether her teaching was in any sense formal. It may only have taken the form of popular persuasion built on unexamined assumptions."[7]

I wholeheartedly agree with his statement. Frankly, I know few Christians who will assert that they are *knowingly* choosing to adopt compromise because of a well-formed doctrine they have embraced. Far more often than not, it is simply a case of naïve, inattentive Christians who have lost the discipline of daily comparing what they are being taught with the Word of God.

One cannot know the motivation of those who choose the path of accommodation, but I suspect that they don't want to offend or they are fearful of being singled out. Christian scholars don't want to be marginalized or ridiculed. Pastors don't want to be perceived as extreme. Christians have adopted a stance which is no stance at all…all the while professing to follow a Lord who has said some very precise things about our relationship with the world.

Still wanting to "eyeball it," and perhaps motivated by the fear of man's disapproval, progressive Christian bridge builders today continue to add piece after piece of speculation. They even tie the pieces together in a seeming successful ways. It certainly looks like it is a legitimate bridge—that is until crunch time. Does the bridge actually reach people in such a fashion that people cross over to a personal relationship with the God of the Bible on God's terms? Or have they merely had some religious cosmetic smeared on lifestyles they have no intention of changing?

How did we get to a place like this? Why the seeming desperation? Why so quick to apologize for the Bible and what it says? Does Jesus need a makeover? Does the church need to respond to every poll or survey?

Don't pay attention to the duck

A canard is a story—usually a damaging story—that's false, but purports to be true. It can be a rumor, a hoax, or an out and out lie.... *Canard comes from the French word for duck...* so how do we get from ducks to an absurd baseless rumor? The *Oxford Dictionary* cites an old expression to describe a scheme or a hoax that means "to sell half a duck." Clearly you can't sell half a duck, or at least not half a live duck, so presumably the story is about a seller who cheated a buyer by selling only half a duck."[8]

A canard is a *scheme.*

I am not a hunter. I have no big issue with hunting, I just never experienced it growing up. I have, however, known lots of people who do hunt. One who comes to mind is a pastor friend from my years in Canada. The area where he lived and served in Saskatchewan is known for its duck hunting. I was always amazed to hear Pastor Earl Millar's stories. I was impressed at the commitment and the lengths to which he would go to bag his limit.

He told me that some hunters actually go out into grain fields and lie in a field, their shotgun at the ready, and cover themselves up with hay or stalks of grain...they lie there silently until they can lure the duck to land in that field. They then pop up from their cover and blast away.

Others buy expensive ATVS and take their decoys deep into the woods to place them in a pond and just wait till they can "call" the ducks and hope the ducks will come down from the sky…thinking that they are landing in safety near others of their denomination. (That's a stretch I know…but I'm a preacher.)

Still others use a "blind," a pre-positioned vantage point, from which they can with sufficient cover get a good shot. It is interesting to me that Paul said that in the case of the unbelieving, "the god of this age has *blinded the minds* of unbelievers, so they cannot see the light of the gospel that displays the glory of Christ…" (2 Cor. 4:4). The Greek word Paul used which is translated blindness does not refer to a total inability to see, but rather refers to state of obscuring the truth—clouding it so that things are not seen as definite and distinguishable.[9]

What I am going to say next may appear too simplistic for some and too confrontational for others. I believe that the whole notion of post modernism—all the books, all the conferences, all the time spent on studying it may be a canard… a scheme. I say this because frankly I disagree with what the church is doing in response to postmodern presuppositions.

The main bone I have to pick with those who write on this subject is this. Wittingly or unwittingly they voice the same assumptions loud and clear.

In virtually everything I have read from church leaders to do with post modernism, something like this is said:

- The church has been not only ineffective, but irrelevant
- Post-moderns are different
- Therefore we must adapt the message and the way we convey it to something more palatable to their tastes.

Donald Miller author of *Blue Like Jazz* was featured on the cover of *Christianity Today.*

"Miller," they wrote, *"is a bridge builder"* to an irreverent, bohemian world. His work is framed with bohemia—a road trip, a pint of beer, an occasional cuss word—but filled with explicit longing for Jesus. He never talks on basic Christian tenets or evangelical priorities such as biblical authority or spreading the gospel."[10]

Really? He *never* talks on basic tenets or biblical authority or spreading the gospel? I beg to differ. David Dunlap in his critique of Donald Miller and *Blue Like Jazz* points out that Campus Crusade for Christ has purchased 65,000 copies of his book to include it their Freshman Survival Kits. Why would they do that?

Could it be that it was precisely because Miller not only addresses basic Christian tenets, but frames them in such a fashion so as to coach the incoming freshmen in the art of downplaying the certainty of the claims of Christ? This is an attractive idea. The new frosh won't "stick out" or face controversy.

Miller in his book, and the movie that followed, intentionally sets out to influence his audience in such a way that will leave the impression that the Church "as is" is not only irrelevant, but that it is necessary for the church to apologize to the culture for our insistence that there are absolutes and standards of holiness. He is advocating for something, alright. Whether or not it is the faith once for all delivered to the saints, let the reader decide.

Dunlap points out that author Dave Hunt's *The Berean Call*, Roger Oakland's *Faith Undone* and *Understanding the Times,* John MacArthur's *The Truth War,* and Dr. Douglas Groothius, professor of philosophy of Denver Seminary have all sounded the alarm about the teaching of Donald Miller in *Blue Like Jazz*.

Dunlap goes on to quote Miller who describes his view of Christian spirituality:

"For me the beginning of my sharing my faith with people began by throwing out Christianity and embracing Christian spirituality, a non-political mysterious system that can be experienced but not explained." This emphasis of experience over doctrine is all through emergent church writings. I personally believe that the reason this resonates with people is that no one's experience can be said to be normative, or no one's "take" on truth can be said to be either right or wrong.[11]

I think David Dunlap has it right when he concludes, "Donald Miller overplays the Christianity-stinks-but-Jesus-is-cool card a little too much."[12]

Citing the Catholic confessional stunt that Dan Merchant used in his documentary, *Lord Save Us from Your Followers*, toward the end of Merchant's film—which by the way has an almost identical set of Emergent talking points—there is a scene in which he set up a faux Catholic confessional in which He "confessed the sins of the Church" against gays at the "Pride" celebration in Portland, Oregon. Dunlap reminds us that this was first tried at Reed College where the same confessional idea was used in which Donald Miller's friend "confessed the sins of the church" to the students at one of the most liberal, hedonistic institutions in America.

Dunlap says:

> In *Blue Like Jazz* he [Miller] wants to invite the readers to authentic Christian spirituality, although he is not really sure what it looks like. He can only report what he has experienced—and it has been a confusing journey! This means that some of his readers will walk away even more confused about true Christianity, but more encouraged to get another tattoo or piercing, grow those dreadlocks, attend another anti-Bush protest, or say another profanity. They will learn that watching South Park is not bad, that having crushes on lesbian pop stars is cool, and that smoking marijuana is unimportant to God.[13]

An unbelieving friend tells Miller that she does not understand why he believes in God or why he insists she must also. He responds by saying, "I don't know why either… but I believe in God, Laura. There is something inside that causes me to believe." He then compares it to "belief in Peter Pan or the Tooth Fairy," or the feeling of love, or the experience of beauty. It is "feeling"—a supra-logical sensation of beauty—that is the basis of his belief.

Miller would like Christians to stop voicing their opposition to abortion, to homosexuality, pornography and other cultural sins of the day. He opposes George W. Bush and the Republican Party and argues that conservative Christians have made a wreck of the evangelical Church."[14]

This argument is almost identical to sentiments that would later be articulated in Jonathan Merritt's book, *A Faith of Their Own.* In that book Merritt, appealing to the same constituency as Miller does, also discourages any overt opposition to abortion or gay rights... as unseemly. After lecturing us that Christians ought to be disengaged politically and refrain from opposing abortion on demand and gay marriage, Donald Miller himself actively hit the campaign trail using his newfound celebrity to reelect a president who has publically affirmed his support of both issues.

I find it fascinating that David Dunlap wrote these words in 2008... the same year that Donald Miller was invited to give an invocation at the Democratic National Convention...the one that nominated the then Senator Barack Obama. The "invocation" consisted of a predictable set of Democratic talking points. This is the same party that would, four years later in 2012, take a public stand in favor of:

- Gay marriage
- Abortion on demand, supported and funded by the federal government
- The abandonment of support for the recognition of Jerusalem being the capital of Israel

William Paul Young, another Portland writer, in his novel *The Shack* has the character "Papa" (his depiction of God the Father) saying the following to Mack, the main character of the novel, "I am not who you think I am.... I don't need to punish people for their sin.... .Sin is its own punishment. It's not my purpose to punish it; it is my joy to cure it.... God cannot send any of his children to an eternity of hell just because they sin against him."[15]

In rapid-fire sequence Young challenges:

- The self-revelation of God found in the Bible...for it is there we find out who Father God is and what He is like
- The universal condition of man and what the Bible says about sin
- God the Holy Spirit's revelation to the Apostle Paul regarding punishment for rejecting God

The Apostle Paul wrote to the Thessalonians:

God is just. He will pay back trouble to those who trouble you, and give relief to those who are troubled, and to us as well. This will happen when the Lord Jesus is revealed from heaven in blazing fire with his powerful angels. *He will punish those who do not know God, and who do not obey the gospel of our Lord Jesus.* They will be punished with everlasting destruction and shut out from the presence of the Lord and from the majesty of his might on the day he comes to be glorified in his holy people and to be marveled at among all those who have believed (2 Thess. 1:6-10, emphasis mine).

What is confusing about that? Paul is forthright and loving in speaking God's Word. It is crystal clear that Emergent Church leaders and sympathetic authors have taken it upon themselves to use the postmodernism canard to springboard to their real agenda, to promote "another gospel" complete with a less offensive god who doesn't ruffle the sensitive feathers of those deemed to be postmodern.

Pastor after pastor buys the premise that this ethereal group known as post-moderns are so different, so fragile, that we dare not confront them. Yes, I used the word *confront*, with the claims of Christ and the standards of a holy God.

It all reminds me of a tragic scene I watched unfold years ago at a hospital where I worked as an orderly. A young man came in to have exploratory surgery. Doctors suspected cancer. After the surgery, the doctors told the family that the mass was indeed cancerous, and had metastasized to the point where nothing more could be done. The man was going to die.

His family determined that he couldn't handle the truth about his condition. We were instructed to take care of him exactly as before and just speak encouragingly to him. Never under any circumstance were we to acknowledge how sick he was.

I remember how awful it was when I bathed him and dressed the surgical wound. He would smile and say "Look at the incision…it's pink… I'm healing…I'm getting better…" All the while I knew that inside him was a rapidly spreading cancer that would soon take his life.

I feel that way about this whole canard that people in our day need a specialized, sanitized, homogenized, gluten-free gospel which is no gospel at all. The Bible says that the ones who do not know Jesus as their Savior are lost. We do them no favor to downplay that essential fact. Telling them the truth as it is found in Jesus (see Eph. 4:21) is the right thing to do.

I mentioned that a canard has been defined as a *scheme.* In his letter to the Ephesians, Paul from prison exhorts the believers to "take up the full armor of God so that they can take a stand against the devil's schemes." The Greek word for "scheme," *methodias,* is where we get our word methodical.

I believe that the Devil's scheme is a methodical assault on the very notion of such a thing as propositional truth, because in that truth is found the only way of salvation, and the Devil is a destroyer who is described as one actively "seeking whom he may devour." Perhaps he won't need to devour if he can successfully distract. A canard can be an effective distraction.

I was on a treadmill at the gym watching the 2012 Summer Games in London. This particular day they were covering the women's marathon swim. This endurance race is typically held in a river or a canal or a bay. In London it was held in Hyde Park.

As in any marathon, the pack begins to narrow until at the end the leaders actually begin to sprint to the finish. The course actually narrows into a taper that will allow only one racer to touch the finish line. As I watched the race, three or four racers went all out at the end.

One woman was clearly ahead when the announcer said, "Did you see it?" The cameraman cut to the most unlikely distraction I'd ever seen in an Olympic event...*there was a duck*...right in the middle of the last turn. The leader began to veer wide at that turn and almost lost the race! Diverting her attention for just a moment almost cost her everything. The most fascinating part of this whole incident was the name of the venue where the race was held. It was known as *Serpentine Lake!*[16]

Like the serpent of old, the Devil would love nothing better than for the church, which Paul describes as the pillar of the truth (see 1 Tim. 3:15), to become distracted just enough at just the right juncture of the race. Dealing with the duck is just enough to take us off course.

I suppose it should come as no surprise that this same devil would have some of his minions—demons—involved in teaching doctrines. No, I did not say that Emergent teachers are demons. I am saying, though, that demonic doctrines exist, and the purpose of these doctrines may be to distract, cloud up, and ultimately deter people from the truth.

A bridge, even a bridge to a bohemian culture, still needs to be engineered according to specifications that are reliable.

A BRIDGE MUST BE MADE OF TESTED MATERIALS

I grew up in Youngstown, Ohio, famous for steel mills, athletes, and mobsters, not necessarily in that order. I actually worked in a steel mill one summer. My job title was "mason's helper." That meant my job was to throw bricks to a brick mason who was rebuilding the open hearth furnace that was being repaired. We were never far from other furnaces that were still operating at the time, so it was hot! The safety officer passed out salt pills so that the workers wouldn't pass out.

The Bible says, "Every Word of God is true...refined in a furnace seven times on the ground" (Ps. 12:6). This verse has resonated with me because of my experience at the mill. It describes the process by which metal is forged and tested. It is meant to convince the reader of the trustworthiness of *every* Word of God.

The metal used in bridges is tested first to see if it can withstand the forces that will come against it. God's Word has been tested often throughout history. The trustworthiness and reliability of the Word of God has survived the fire, yet even still in our generation there are attempts to discredit its authenticity, reliability, and relevance.

The importance of taking salt pills was also driven home to me. It got so hot in the open hearth area that it was not unusual to lose eight to ten pounds in a shift. The reason we needed to take salt pills was the fact that the electrolyte balance of the human body can be dangerously affected by such extreme heat. In some instances a person under such heat stress could pass out or worse…suffer a heart attack or stroke.

I suffered from heat exhaustion once. While playing basketball outdoors in the ninety-five degree heat one muggy day, I got disoriented and dizzy. I vomited. I wasn't able to string two thoughts together.

Our bodies are made to precise chemical specifications. The human body is made up of exactly .09 saline fluid. This is why such a solution serves as an ideal medium through which to introduce medicines into a hospital patient's body. In the ER the phrase, "Get a line started," meant that the nurse was to start an IV with a solution that was comprised of liquid made from a solution that is exactly .09 saline.

Jesus said, "You are the salt of the earth." Paul said we are to live in such a fashion that our conversation (even a postmodern conversation) should be literally "seasoned with salt" (Col. 4:6). Emergent church literature is replete with the term *conversation*. That term is, I suppose, meant to imply a no-threat approach, but it is also implies that there is no final outcome. What Paul meant by "conversation" was that our *manner of behavior* should be such that there ought to be correct balance. For our purposes of discussion I can say, "Yes we should use creative ways to engage the culture, but only in exact proportion to the fixed truth of God's Word."

Paul said that we were to have our conversation (manner of life as well as our mere words) seasoned with salt. Back to the IV solution illustration, I preached on this subject a number of times over the years, and I always made the point that the *feelings* of love we feel for people must be in exact proportion with the *fixed truth* of God's Word. I reminded people that the bag of IV fluid you see hung on the pole is actually called "Normal Saline."

God's truth is propositional whether we prefer it or not. It is normative…and "normal" in every sense. In order for people to be truly healed they need for us to be forthright in both our feelings *and* the unchangeable truth of God's Word—all of it…not just the passages that are deemed least offensive to postmodern sensibilities.

To attempt to build a bridge in order to reach the lost which has not been built of time-tested, tempered steel is to surrender to mere accommodation and to court disaster. To fail to maintain a balance of truth and love is to expose ourselves to impaired reasoning and the possibility of fainting in the heat of the day.

A BRIDGE HAS TO BE INSPECTED PERIODICALLY AND PROPERLY MAINTAINED

When I think about this, I think how entire denominations that used to be considered conservative just thirty years ago are now flirting with doctrines that undermine the very founding principles which brought them into existence. Seminaries used to require faculty and students to sign on the dotted line that they agreed with the basic doctrinal position of the school.

Now some of these institutions have faculty members who do not believe in the bodily resurrection of Jesus, the virgin birth, and the inerrancy of Scriptures. Imagine, seminary professors holding forth on campuses that were founded by men who would be aghast at the apostate climate of the schools they founded.

I ask, what would be lost if seminaries once again held their faculties to a standard in keeping with their original statements of belief? What would happen if denominational authorities insisted that their credentialed ministers annually sign a document in which they affirm that they are in full agreement with the doctrinal positions of that body? What would happen if dissenters were asked to leave? The short answer is that no one will know until some school or some denomination takes the bold step of insisting on doctrinal compliance again.

I don't know much about engineering, but I do know what happens when bridges fail. There is a public outcry, and politicians look for someone to blame. "Why wasn't this bridge regularly inspected?" Nobody seems offended by the notion of someone getting fired then; they expect it!

Over time, the simple wear and tear of use, abuse, and weather can degrade a bridge to the point of danger. When I consider this, I am reminded that just because a church, a pastor, or a professor *used to be* conservative and sound theologically, that the person still adheres to a rock solid affirmation of the inerrancy of Scripture.

I think it would be profitable for ministers to periodically preach a series of messages with a title like "The Faith Once for All Delivered to the Saints." It would serve to make each minister face his or her current beliefs. Are they still in alignment, or has there occurred what some have labeled "mission creep?"

THE BRIDGES OF GOD BETTER BE "OF GOD"

Sadly, it is possible to be inordinately proud of the bridge we have engineered simply because it was the result of our own inventiveness. It is possible that even if one day we learned that the enemy was using the bridge we ourselves have designed…using it to attack us…we would still fight any attempt to dismantle what we have built in our own strength.

Sound implausible? One of the greatest war movies of all time is *The Bridge on the River Kwai.* Sir Alec Guinness plays the part of a British Commander of a group of POWs who are being forced by their Japanese captors to build a railway bridge for the purpose of advancing the war effort of the enemy.

William Holden plays a new prisoner who hasn't been in captivity long enough to become assimilated into the reality of being a slave laborer. He escapes. He later returns to sabotage the bridge. There is an extremely poignant scene where, on the day of dedication of the bridge, the Holden character sneaks back and wires the structure with explosives, and buries the detonating wire in the sand.

Just as the first troop train approaches, the Japanese commander is about to discover the wire. Holden, who is hiding on the opposite beach, gets Guinness' attention from across the river. Guinness looks puzzled. He figures out that the bridge has been wired. Holden gestures to Guinness to "Kill the Japanese commander!" Guinness pauses, refusing to let the bridge he built be destroyed, even though the train that would soon cross the bridge was bringing more Japanese soldiers who would kill more Allied soldiers.

Think of it—tenacity in defense of something we have embraced, even in the face of evidence that the enemy may be using it!

DO WE DESIGN AND BUILD THE BRIDGE OR ARE WE "IN" THE BRIDGE?

Never in my life have I been more acutely aware of the high stakes involved with bridging the gap to those who need Jesus than in September of 2001. At the time, I was serving as the reserve chaplain to the Thirteenth Coast Guard District. When I, with all of you, saw the second plane hit the twin towers of The World Trade Center, I watched in horror. Somehow, I just knew I was going to go to Ground Zero.

The next day I called the chaplain of The Coast Guard's office and volunteered. The Chaplains Emergency Response Team was formed, and within ten days I was packing for my trip to Manhattan.

Just recently, I remembered an incident that took place involving one of my chaplain colleagues at Ground Zero. The team was billeted at a Coast Guard facility on Staten Island. Each day we would travel by van across the Verrazano Bridge to spend the day in three distinct capacities:

1. For the first third of the day we ministered to the rescue/recovery workers at "The Pile."
2. Then we were transported to the Morgue where we ministered to the incredible teams of forensic workers who came to identify bodies… and body parts.
3. We would end the day ministering to the family members who had lost colleagues, friends, or family.

As we traveled to Ground Zero each day, I began to take notice of one particular Catholic chaplain who I didn't know very well. As the van would pass the concrete base of the Verrazano Bridge, He would make the sign of the cross and utter a quiet prayer. One day, we were seated near each other and I asked him, "Father, I don't mean to pry, but I noticed you making the sign of the cross every time we pass this spot. May I ask if there is something special about this particular spot?"

"My friend is there."

"Oh, does he work on the bridge?"

"No, he is *in* the bridge...."

He went on to tell me that a friend of his family died as the result of an accident during the construction of the Verrazano Bridge and that his body was never recovered. Most probably his remains were actually entombed in the structure of the bridge. I never looked at that bridge the same way for the entire time we were there.

After remembering this incident, I decided to do a little research about the building of the Verrazano Bridge. It turns out there were in fact four fatalities during the construction of the bridge.

Author Gay Talese wrote a book entitled *The Bridge*. The publisher, Random House, in their profile of the author describes Talese's preparation:

> From the shore's edge Talese watched barges carrying loads of steel, and as he watched he wanted to know what it was like to be a bridge builder, "to be up there courting danger while building something that is going to outlive you, as all great bridges outlive the people who create them...."

Chapter 6 of *The Bridge* is titled "Death on the Bridge," and here Gerard McKee, a handsome popular youth from a boomer (a boomer is a transient worker, especially in bridge construction) family falls to his death from the Verrazano span. Gerard has two brothers who are also boomers, and his father—a man whom Gerard strongly resembled—had been hit by a collapsing crane a few years before, had his leg permanently twisted, had a steel plate inserted in his head, and was disabled for life.

Of all the mourners at Gerard's funeral, his father suffers most. "After what I've been through," he said, shaking his head with tears in his eyes, "I should know enough to keep my kids off the bridge." But McKee doesn't, and *The Bridge* ends with another son's death on the next bridge project.[17]

I wept as I read that gripping tale of one family's incredible loss. I thought about the potential risk involved in building a bridge, and how that risk can affect more than one generation.

As I considered all of this in respect to this whole topic of building bridges, I was reminded of a line from a Robert Frost poem I memorized in high school:

> Before I built a wall I'd ask to know…what I was walling in or walling out…and to whom I was like to give offence…[18]

As I thought about his question, I asked one of my own. Before I build or attempt to build a bridge, should I not first be settled as to who it is I am attempting to reach and what it is I am trying to reach them with… and who I am willing to offend by my efforts? I considered those questions and a few more.

What is an acceptable "offense"? Do I choose to risk offending the people I am trying to reach with the gospel that is, by God's own definition, an "offense" and a "stumbling block," or am I more willing to risk offending the God in whose name I attempt to build bridges?

How one answers that question matters. Will I simply "try out" a few new approaches that are currently in vogue that cost me nothing, or will I risk giving my life in becoming part of the bridge myself? Is the bridge something I fabricate, or am I myself *in* the bridge?

Will the bridges we build survive our efforts? Will people suffer harm because we are improvising? Are the materials we use time-tested and engineered according to specifications?

It matters.

It matters a lot.

Six

ABOUT THE TRUSTWORTHINESS OF INSTRUMENTS

I remember a remark overheard at a pastors' conference. The speaker was lamenting the fact that he had sent some of his young leaders to a particular seminary. He lamented, "It is as if we were to set a group of small children adrift at sea...or to leave them lost in the woods without a compass or the knowledge of how to use one."

As a prerequisite to serving as a chaplain to the Marines, I first needed to complete a course in which we learned battle skills. One of the skills we needed to learn was land navigation.

We were given a compass, a protractor, and a map. The exercise was devised to teach us how to find a series of objectives using only these three tools. It is not difficult to see how important it is for anyone in the heat of battle to find out where he is and where he is going. It is vital that he not only know how to use, but also trust, the instruments that will get him from point A to point B.

I was at Camp Lejeune, North Carolina, in July. As the chiggers feasted on my flesh and the sweat poured off my already soaked BDUs, we were each paired with another chaplain. I scored. I just happened to be paired with a man who had previously served as an infantry soldier in Vietnam. We had a quick class on the protractor and the compass, and learned about terms like "azimuth."

Then, each pair of chaplains was dropped off in the middle of nowhere with a map, the compass, the protractor, and a set of pre-ordained objectives we were to meet. We labored in the heat and found the first marker by the prescribed method. I kept asking my new BFF Chaplain for his "advice"— translation: Would you do this please? I'm already lost.

After we had been at it for a few hours in the hot North Carolina sun getting acquainted with ticks and dodging snakes, we came up with a plan. I was more than willing to do the leg work if he would do the skill part; actually reading the map, using the compass and protractor, and finding the marks. It made sense. He did his part and I did mine and we finished before all the other chaplains. I actually had myself convinced that this was a clever use of teamwork.

There was one minor problem, though. I never learned to do it myself. Fortunately, I was never placed in a situation where I had to use those skills; but had I been thrust into harm's way out in the middle of nowhere, I would have become a liability to the Marines in that they would have to come and find me if I got lost.

I have wondered many times since that hot muggy day about what the next generation of Christians will look like if they never learn to find their way in the Lord because they haven't the instruments, or worse, they no longer trust *the* instrument, the Word of God—the Scriptures.

You have to have land navigation skills because when that GPS goes down—and it will—you have to know what to do next. Malfunctioning equipment, downed satellites or dead batteries could leave Marines stuck. Those in leadership especially need to know how to navigate by traditional and reliable means.[1]

This quote appeared in the July 9, 2012, issue of the *Marine Corps Times* which featured two articles by Gina Harkins showing the seriousness of not learning how to navigate—or worse relying on someone else to navigate for you. The first article, entitled, "Kicked Out… Record number of OCS candidates booted amid cheating allegations," chronicles the sad tale of the dismissal of twenty one officer candidates:

Staff members at Officer Candidates School dismissed the largest group of prospective Marines in the training program's history after 31 members were thought to have cheated on a night navigation exam.

Candidates said a storm pushed the land nav. test back by several hours, so cloud coverage and the late time of night made the course more difficult to navigate than it had been during their practice run. They said they were told not to talk during the exam, but it wasn't talking that got them into trouble—it was tapping on the ammunition cans that lined the course, alerting other candidates to their positions.

Only two candidates were found to be actually tapping on the boxes. But even those who heard the sounds and let it impact their decision-making during the exam were labeled cheaters. Stillings said that as potential officers, they should have told someone that something wrong was happening on the course, and no one did.[2]

In the second article entitled "Navigating by a Compass in the Age of GPS? Why Bother?" Harkins shows why this was such a big deal:

Col. Kris Stillings, commanding officer at OCS, said land nav. is still an important skill for Marines to know. It goes beyond their school and even the Marine Corps. It's one of those bedrock skills that any member of the military has to have....

"GPS is a wonderful tool, but like any kind of technology, it's only a tool," Stillings said. "You have to have land navigation skills because when that GPS goes down—and it will—you have to know what to do next. Malfunctioning equipment, downed satellites or dead batteries could leave Marines stuck. *Those in leadership especially need to know how to navigate by traditional and reliable means.*" [Emphasis mine.]

Harkins cites a valuable lesson learned in Iraq:

In 2009, one sergeant at the Battle Skills Training School at Camp Lejeune shared with his students a valuable lesson he learned while deployed. Former Sgt. Damian Senerchia warned his students not to become reliant on technology to find their way around.

On a winter day in 2005, Senerchia's infantry squad suddenly found itself lost among a series of buildings and alleyways in Hit, Iraq. The Marines' GPS receiver went blank during a foot patrol. They had a map, but no extra batteries and no compass.

"We were using the GPS as our compass," said Senerchia, then a Private First Class. "It put us in a bad position, especially in that urban environment. We didn't know where we were."

Once they called for help, and a Quick Reaction Force found them, they realized they were less than 10 minutes from their base. It was an embarrassing story, but he used it to impress upon his students that knowing how to use old-school navigation techniques is crucial.

"When that technology goes, what do you have?" Senerchia asked. "Without these skills, you're sitting ducks. You have to keep doing it and keep doing it and keep doing it. It's very perishable."[3]

I feel that many pastors have lost a crucial skill... that of knowing how to use the Scripture as the basis for *all* of our theological reflection. Sadly, like the "land nav." skills learned in boot camp, such skills are lost because we have lost our confidence in our instrument—the Bible. Our trust is too easily extinguished over time. Instead of relying on the time-honored Word of God, we have trusted in the latest technologies of men. When they go down, and they will go down, how will we be able to lead people if we ourselves are lost?

I have two friends who are pilots. I asked each of them how pilots are trained to navigate in low visibility or in storms. They both cited the absolute necessity of being *instrument rated*. Dr. Roy Hicks Sr. wrote a small book years ago that described the necessity for the believer to be *instrument rated*. The book is titled *Ready or Not Here Comes Trouble*.

Dr. Hicks begins by describing what it is like to be lost in a storm:

The lost pilot and the troubled Christian have something in common. Both could sail along life's pathway smoothly until the storm came. They were not ready for the troubles they encountered. They are typical of many who do not make the special effort who do not have that special dedication to prepare for that which all will inevitably face...the storms of life.[4]

He goes on to show what the problem is:

There are literally thousands of pilots who learn to fly a small plane. They can take off, maneuver, and land it. They can do this successfully as long as they can see where they are going. They can find their way, going by the landmarks, rivers, mountains, lakes and highways, but when they are socked in by storms and cannot see, they will be overcome by vertigo.

You see there is a sensitive device in our heads that can be likened to a carpenter's level. The force of motion of spinning will send the bubble as far as it goes to one side. When it can go no further, it begins to return...even though the person may still be spinning in the same direction. Thus he has the sensation of stopping and beginning to spin in the opposite direction. But it is only a sensation and in reality he has never changed directions! If he were not blindfolded and could see, he could ignore those sensations and would have no difficulty in knowing what direction he was going.[5]

The remedy for spiritual vertigo is surprisingly simple.

To be ready for the storms of life... means that one must be prepared by spending hours in the Word. This is the instrument of the Christian walk. Great familiarity with it is necessary if the Christian is to be "certified" to navigate all the storms of life.

When a regularly licensed pilot who has a private license desires to go to the instrument rated license, he must apply and be ready to begin hours and hours of study. Then an instructor is assigned to him who will accompany him on his training missions.

The instructor will place a hood (a long-billed cap) on the pilot's head so that all the pilot can see is the instrument panel in front of him. This is all he could see if were actually flying in storm conditions or a fog. This is done after the craft is in the air for a few hundred feet. A course is set and the pilot in training must work his instruments and radio doing many turns, being able to come to an airport and bring the plane within a few feet of the landing strip. This simulated blindness, causing confusion to the average person, is soon overcome by disciplined training. The flights "under the hood" (as the procedure is called) become merely routine flights.[6]

Dr. Hicks concludes,

Jesus…pronounced a great blessing on all who would believe without their natural sense being involved…upon those who are instrument rated…who do not live by what they see or feel, but what the Bible, our instrument book, says.[7]

My pilot friend, Steve Aveldson, heard me use this illustration in a sermon. He got me aside and said, "Pastor Jim, don't forget that there is more to that whole topic." He reminded me that the instruments themselves regularly need to be calibrated to "true north."

Seafarers know what this all about. If you can find the Morning Star, you can get the needed first reference point with which to orient yourself. How and where do we find the "True North," the real Jesus, His real words? Are we left to our own devices?

Perhaps it is simply a matter of recognizing our innate "lostness" and confessing our need for guidance at every turn. Dr. Roy Hicks quoted a pilot who told him, "Recently a pilot told me that the more he *had* to depend on his instruments, the more confidence he had in them."

I once toured the then new fifty-foot motor lifeboat rolled out by the Coast Guard. This new model replaced the old forty-seven footer, and had lots of high-tech goodies. I spoke with a senior chief who confided that he was glad for all the high tech additions, but wished that there was more redundancy. "What happens if all this stuff is rendered inoperable... then what?"

I ask a similar question to those who dismiss the inerrancy of the Bible. If the Bible is thought to contain both inspired passages and human error, then what? Who decides which is which and what criteria will they use?

J.I. Packer wrote,

> So the decision facing Christians today is simply this: Will we take our lead at this point from Jesus and the apostles? Will we let ourselves be guided by a Bible received as inspired and therefore wholly true (for God is not the author of untruths), or will we strike out, against our Lord and his most authoritative representatives, on a line of our own?
>
> If we do, we have already resolved in principle to be led not by the Bible as given but by the Bible as we edit and reduce it. We are then likely to be found before long scaling down its mysteries (for example, incarnation and atonement) and relativizing its absolutes (for example, in sexual ethics) in the light of our own divergent ideas.

He goes on to show that once we acquiesce at this important point it is inevitable that we will miss an important lesson:

> And in that case Psalm 119 will stand as an everlasting rebuke to us, for instead of doubting and discounting some things in his Bible, the psalmist prayed for understanding so that he might live by God's law. (Law here means not just commands but all authoritative instruction that bears on living.) This is the path of true reverence, true discipleship and true enrichment.

But once we entertain the needless and unproved, indeed unprovable notion that Scripture cannot be fully trusted, that path is partly closed to us. Therefore it is important to maintain inerrancy and to counter denials of it, for only so can we keep open the path of consistent submission to biblical authority and consistently concentrate on the true problem, that of gaining understanding without being entangled in the false question of how much of Scripture should we disbelieve. [8]

If you were lost in a combat area, which option would you choose? Rely on Chaplain Jenkins' intuition, or trust your instruments and your ability to use them? Would you prefer that the person in the cockpit of the plane carrying your family is instrument rated, or would you be satisfied to know that he or she is up on the latest cultural trends?

I'm just asking…

SEVEN

CONFORMING TO THE CROSS OR CALIBRATING TO THE CULTURE?

Leonard Sweet is a name which shows up on virtually every Emergent Church site. He has written numerous books with a common theme running throughout. His theology at points appears to be much more of a New Age amalgam than "the faith once for all delivered to the saints." Here is a sample from his book *Quantum Spirituality*:

> So far the church has refused to dip its toe into postmodern culture. A quantum spirituality challenges the church to bear its past and to dare its future by sticking its big TOE into the time and place of the present…. Then, and only then, will the church not appear to be in a time capsule…sealed against new developments.
>
> Then, and only then, will a New Light movement of "world-making" faith have helped to create the world that is to, and may yet, be. Then, and only then, will earthlings have uncovered the meaning of these words, some of the last words poet/activist/contemplative/bridge between East and West Thomas Merton uttered: "We are already one. But we imagine that we are not. And what we have to recover is our original unity."[1]

I find it fascinating that he refers to Thomas Merton as a "contemplative bridge between East and West." As I previously noted today there are scores of Contemplative Spirituality courses being offered in heretofore conservative seminaries that in the fairly recent past would have eschewed any attempt to bridge the gap between East (mysticism) and West (propositional truth).

Here is a simple question. Were the Hebrews to "be one" with the Philistines? Are we all one and the same when it comes to ultimate truth? Does the Old Testament record the Lord endorsing any attempt to syncretize and harmonize the different religions? Is Jesus the same as Mohammed or Buddha?

I remember a quote from Dr. John Warwick Montgomery. He said in a class lecture that, "A universe in which Roman Catholicism and Unitarianism could both be universally true would be a madhouse."[2]

I won't take the time to dwell on Dr. Sweet's New Age imagery. His own words reveal his sympathies with elements of a movement that at its inception actually lauded Lucifer. (Research the origins of The New Age Movement. An in depth study will yield fascinating statements by Madame Blavatsky and David Spangler, and will show the ties to Lucis Trust.) You, my reader, decide if it is significant that a seminary professor at a so-called evangelical school is teaching this material. How do you feel about a Christian theologian who cites things like this?

The following quote appears in Sweet's *Quantum Spirituality*:

Rabbi/theologian/storyteller Lawrence Kushner makes an intriguing contrast between the Jewish and Christian traditions precisely at this point in *The River of Light Spirituality, Judaism, and the Evolution of Consciousness.*

"For Christianity, the central problem is how God could have become person. How spirit could transform itself into matter… Word become flesh… consciousness become protoplasm. The direction is from the top down. For Judaism, on the other hand, the problem is how humanity could possibly attain to God's word and intention. How matter could raise itself to spirit. How simple desert souls could hear the word. Human substance attain…consciousness. The intention is "to permeate matter and raise it to spirit." The direction is from the bottom up. Perhaps the two traditions, one moving down, the other moving up, are destined to meet in the divinity of humanity."[3] [Note: I am aware these are not Dr. Sweet's remarks, but he quotes them in a favorable context.]

If that sounds a little like Gnosticism, it is. The idea that man has innate divinity and is being raised to another level of consciousness is not new. Much of the Gnostic heresy that the early church fathers faced had just such notions. Listen to the overtly New Age overtones in this remark:

Quantum spirituality is more than a structure of the intellect; it is more than a structure of emotion; it is more than a structure of human being. It is most importantly a structure of human becoming, a channeling of Christ energies through mind-body experience.[4] (This *is* directly from Dr. Sweet and his choice of words here evokes sympathy to New Age notions of the human fusion with divinity.)

The divinity of humanity…? A channeling of "Christ energies" through mind-body experiences?

Leonard Sweet has shared the platform with Rick Warren. He was invited to address the worship leader conference for Calvary Chapel hosted by Chuck Smith's nephew. Sometimes his militancy in regard to changing the church is evident.

Change or be changed – In the old ecology of nature, change was seen as abnormal. In the new ecology of nature, change is life's natural, normative state…. What works today won't work tomorrow…. The wonder is that churches are not in more disarray…. They are standing pat, opting to uphold the status quo rather than undergo the upheaval…. Postmodern culture is a change-or-be-changed world. The word is out: Reinvent yourself for the 21st century or die. [5]

I was very interested in his take on how the church needs to be what he calls "in-formed."

According to the *Oxford English Dictionary*, to inform means, "to give form to, put into form and shape." *The purpose of the church is to give form to, to put into form and shape, the energy-matter known as Jesus Christ.* New Light leaders, therefore, are in-formational connectors helping the body of Christ to become an in-formed church, an in-formational community.... New Light leadership helps patches of information become cloaks of knowledge. [Emphasis mine.]

Information brokering is central to creating community in postmodern culture, *not to mention achieving synergic states of group consciousness.* Association of Theological Schools president/divinity school dean Jim L. Waits, in his address at the seventy-fifth anniversary of the founding of Emory University's Candler School of Theology, calls for clergy to move from their "learned ministry" model to a "knowledgeable ministry" model. "Knowledge ministry" helps information become "alive in the consciousness," as Einstein put it.[6] [Emphasis mine.]

Energy matter "known as" Jesus Christ? Information brokering? Achieving synergistic states of group consciousness?

In 2 Timothy, Paul tells Timothy that he must at all costs hold to the "form" of sound doctrine that he, Paul had given him. He uses a Greek word *hupotuposis. Strong's Greek Dictionary of The New Testament* describes the word this way:

Typification under (after) i.e. a sketch...for imitation: form, pattern

a die as struck...it is also rendered a stamp...or a scar. It has its origins in the idea of a cudgel...beating or pummeling with a stick or a bastinado with repeated blows."[7]

Paul told Timothy "*Hold fast the form* of sound words which thou hast heard of me, in faith and love which is in Christ Jesus. That good thing which was committed unto thee keep (another translation says "guard") by the Holy Ghost which dwelleth in us" (2 Tim. 1:13-14, NIV).

I have tried to picture in my mind the sight of this arthritic, horribly scarred, exhausted man chained like a dog, deserted by his friends, telling his young son in the faith, "Guard the gospel, Timothy."

Why would it need to be guarded? Guarded from whom? From what? Paul reminds Timothy, "It was committed to you."

The word Paul uses to describe Timothy's commission is rendered in a modern version as a "sacred trust." It was committed to Timothy by a man who was one whose body *had been stamped... struck as a die... scarred* by the message he was commissioned to share. He was "informed" by opposing the culture of his day. He had been beaten with rods numerous times. Paul in Second Corinthians tells how many times he was flogged severely, beaten with rods. He was also stoned and left for dead.

Paul says in effect, "You have been given a commission. You have a responsibility. It is on you now." He goes on to tell Timothy, "You must charge them before the Lord that they strive not about words to no profit, but the subverting of the hearers" (2 Tim. 2). The NIV reads, "Keep reminding them of these things. Warn them before God against quarreling about words. It is of no value, and only ruins those who listen." *The word translated "subverted" can mean upended like a ship which has capsized. In other words it can refer to a shipwreck.*

Let us go back to Paul's exhortation to Timothy. Later, in the same letter... the last letter he would write, Paul told Timothy,

> But mark this: There will be terrible times in the last days. People
> will be lovers of themselves, lovers of money, boastful, proud, abu-
> sive, disobedient to their parents, ungrateful, unholy, without love,
> unforgiving, slanderous, without self-control, brutal, not lovers of
> the good, treacherous rash, conceited, lovers of pleasure rather than
> lovers of God (2 Tim. 3:1).

What he says next gives us some inkling as to why he was so upset. He says that not only will people be awful, what will be most egregious of all is the fact that they will all the while keep up some religious appearance while behaving this way.

"Having the *form* of godliness but denying its power." The King James Version renders this passage this way: "Having a form of godliness but denying the power thereof." Paul uses an entirely different word for "form" than the one he used in chapter one in his charge to Timothy to "hold to the form of sound teaching."

The word Paul uses to describe this "form of godliness" in chapter three is the word *morphosin*. This is where we get our concept of "morphing." It is a word that gives the idea of a thing fashioned or fabricated…intentionally shaped—not by blows in order to be imitated—no, but intentionally manipulated, adapted if you will, maybe accommodated is the best word.

If I was to try to describe the difference between what Paul told Timothy to do and what many today attempt in the name of innovation, I would say in the first instance God gives the one and only pattern that is to be imitated without any manipulation or fabrication. In the second instance, the people give themselves the right to morph into whatever model or form that suits their desires. This way they can still behave in an ungodly way yet seem religious.

In 2 Timothy, Paul urges his protégé, "Study to shew thyself approved unto God, a workman that needeth not to be ashamed, rightly dividing the word of truth" (2 Tim. 2:15, KJV). I have been fascinated with this verse over the years. I come back to it again and again. What did Paul mean by the phrase "rightly divide"? The Greek word he uses is *orthotomeo*, which can be translated, "to cut straight," or "to cut in a straight line."

Some commentators have said he was referring to the priest in the temple "rightly dividing…i.e. 'precisely, cutting up' the animals for sacrifice." Some others think he had in mind a steward who "makes proper distribution" to each one under his care of such things as his office and their necessities require.."

Still others believe that Paul was referring to "cutting straight" as referring to a stone mason, or carpenter, a ploughman, *or a road cutter*. Let's talk about that last one:

As truth is a straight line, so must our handling of the truth be straightforward and honest, without shifts or tricks.... Roman roads did not veer all over the countryside zig-zagging with every boundary and accommodating every farmer's field. Rome had one thought in mind when it built roads; to carry troops to and from distant territories directly back to Rome. With these mental pictures before us it is clear that Paul was telling Timothy to deal with the truth straightly...not being turned aside by opinions and theories.

Denominations want their own creeds to be honored, but each creed is a departure, a veering from the truth. The fables of those with "itching ears" (see 2 Tim. 4) would detour the truth. Evangelists are to hew the line, hold a straight course, plumb correctly, align evenly as they preach. *As a road line meets obstacles of forests, rivers, and chasms, a preacher will meet error, opposition, and opinions. These must not deter or detour the faithful preaching in the direction God would have us go.*[8] (Emphasis mine.)

As I read this last quote, I remembered an illustration from The Marine Corps manual that describes land navigation. In one drawing we learned how to position the compass with our cheek:

The Compass-to-Cheek Technique: Fold the cover of the compass containing the sighting wire to a vertical position; then fold the rear sight slightly forward. Look through the rear-sight slot and align the front-sight hairline with the desired object in the distance. Then glance down at the dial through the eye lens to read the azimuth.[9]

I thought as I looked at this drawing about how our instrument, the Bible, needs to be positioned close to our mouths, at our cheek. Before we dare to speak, we must first take the measure of the situation, the lay of the land if you will, using the compass of God's inerrant Word. We must first look through the lens of God's revealed will. We must literally bring our sight into alignment with the instrument sight. Not the other way around! Once the proper relationship exists between user and instrument, then and only then can we trust our findings. Secondarily, we can then use maps which have been made by others using the same instruments.

As I mentioned before, on one of my tours of duty, I served with the Coast Guard. I was working in Ketchikan, Alaska, filling in for my active duty counterpart. I visited an island where they were building a road. It was a joint venture using engineers and crews from different reserve components.

They already had the design. Theirs was not a survey based on opinions. They designed the road based on the pre-ordained starting point, the agreed upon destination, and not the existing landscape. Theirs was a survey in its truest sense that would stake out the boundaries.

It would be oriented by calibrated instruments all based on God's created order. They would decide how to deal with the obstacles they would encounter, then they would literally blast their way through and use the material they blasted to build the road. They had to *cut it straight*.

They then made forms…based on coordinates yielded by their instruments. The material was poured into those forms. The net result would ultimately be a road on which children would one day safely travel to school.

We are free to believe whatever we like. Seminary professors are free to teach whatever they like. They can opine as to what they think about the age in which we live. But Paul told Timothy… and I tell any young preacher who will listen, "You do not have the right to make it up as you go. It is not your gospel. They are not your words. If you add to them or subtract from them you do so not only at your peril, but at the peril of those unfortunate enough to hear you."

We are, as the Church, to remove obstacles to cut a straight road, poured into the ancient forms ordained by God. Any "other" gospel is just a pot-holed path to perdition.

As I mentioned earlier, I lived in the mountains of B.C. for a number of years. One had to quickly adapt to the steep, winding mountain roads and the challenge that sudden bad weather could present. While I was in British Columbia they built a new highway through the mountains called the Coquihalla Highway. It was a much more direct route across the mountains, but it was also much steeper.

Once when I was returning from Vancouver to the interior of British Columbia, I noticed that there was not much traffic on the Coquihalla Highway. In fact, it appeared that mine was the only car on the road.

As I ascended the steep grade toward the summit I noticed that the creeks near the highway were swollen to such an extent that water was lapping over the bridge. As I passed the main stem of the river, it became clear to me that I was witnessing a flood.

My first clue was a fifty-foot spruce tree bobbing down the river like a toothpick. Then I saw the corner of a barn half-submerged in the deluge. But I had nothing to worry about; I was driving a Volkswagen Golf! Seriously, I was terrified as I witnessed the sheer power of a river at flood stage; uprooting and carrying away anything in its path. Later after I reached the summit, I learned that the Highway had been closed by the RCMP, and somehow I got through without being stopped.

What Spurgeon warned about in his day, what Criswell echoed in his challenge to the Southern Baptists, what Schaeffer tried to point out in *The Great Evangelical Disaster*, all of these things have come to pass. Like a flood cascading down a steep grade, the relentless challenges to an inerrant Bible have uprooted what seemed to be stable.

Whole denominations have lost their underpinnings. The basis for our preaching has become compromised to such an extent that just about anything that sounds spiritual passes for the Gospel. Listen to this from a 1997 Leadernet NETFAX:

"Spirituality is in," says Sam Keen, author of *Hymns to an Unknown God*. Is it any wonder that advertising reflects this cultural reality? More and more ads are drawing on the rich possibilities of religious and spiritual schemes. From cars to beverages, and health care to sports teams, we see signs and portents that Madison Avenue has jumped on the spiritual bandwagon.

Religious pundits tell us we are experiencing a "great awakening"—

a prolonged period of religious interest that occurs periodically in American history. But this awakening is different. In the past, great awakenings were largely spurred by religious revivals. The current one reflects an increasing separation of spiritual values from the constraints of dogma and denomination.

"We are experiencing a rise of spiritual individualism and uncorseted spiritual experimentation," says Keen. "The institutions of religion are becoming less important, while the spiritual values, disciplines, and ethics they represent have grown in significance."[10]

We are, I suppose, to be impressed with this observation and make the acceptable adaptation to the new normal, which has meant in recent years, "Preach messages that focus on a generalized spirituality rather than a precise gospel."

What seemed similar to the gospel two hundred years ago has become *another gospel*, and it has now carved out a dangerous new course with shipwrecks washing up on the shore—a testimony to the dangerous nature of theological accommodation to a pagan culture. I believe with all my heart that the answer lies not in exploration of new paradigms, but in humble repentance and a return to dependence on God's Spirit instead of our own cleverness.

EIGHT

COMPASS CALLS AND COUNTER-INFORMATION

As for you, you were dead in your transgressions and sins, in which you used to live when you followed the ways of the world and of the ruler of the kingdom of the air [prince of the power of the air-KJV] the spirit who is now at work in those who are disobedient. All of us also lived among them at one time, gratifying the cravings of our sinful nature and following its desires and thoughts.

EPHESIANS 2:1–3

F. F. Bruce in his commentary on the Book of Ephesians writes that these verses can be referring to "the atmosphere or climate of thought which influences peoples' minds against God. The disobedient (literally 'the sons of disobedience' as in Ephesians 5:6) are rebels against the authority of God, responsive to the promptings of the arch-rebel."[1]

The Greek word translated "air" ("ah yer") used in the phrase "the ruler of the kingdom of the air" carries with it the notion of an "atmosphere." It also can refer to the unconscious nature of our breathing. The intentional creation of a toxic atmosphere can bring about as many, if not more, casualties than bombs and bullets.

In September 2001 when I was part of a team of chaplains who responded to the terrorist attacks on the World Trade Center, I breathed the toxic air at Ground Zero and as a result I now have a number of chronic breathing and reflux problems. I am screened annually to see if cancer has developed. The air was full of carcinogens and other toxic material, but I was unaware that what I was breathing then would still be affecting me today.

There is an atmosphere in the church today that is toxic. This climate of skepticism and questioning and doubt comes not from our Heavenly Father, but I believe from "the father of lies." How has Satan managed to get a whole generation of Christians confused as to the trustworthiness and reliability of their Bibles? I suggest that the "prince of the power of the air" has used state-of-the-art techniques.

He has not changed his basic orientation. He was and is a liar and master manipulator. He has, I believe, gotten an entire generation of Christian leaders committed (wittingly or unwittingly) to a posture of accommodation to a culture that is in rebellion against God.

The whole nature of waging war has dramatically changed in the last few decades. Drones can rain fire down from the skies. Cyber-warfare is now a fact of life. Take this example:

The EC-130 Compass Call aircraft attempts to disrupt enemy command and control communications and limits adversary coordination essential for enemy force management.

The Compass Call system employs offensive counter-information and electronic attack capabilities in support of US and Coalition tactical air, surface, and special operations forces. The EC-130H was used extensively in the Gulf War and Operation Iraqi Freedom, disrupting Iraqi communications at both the strategic and tactical levels. It has also been used in Operation Enduring Freedom in Afghanistan.[2]

When I read that description I thought, *Why was this state-of-the-art weapons delivery system called "Compass Call"?* I also reflected on its purpose which is to employ "Offensive counter-information and electronic attack capabilities."

In light of what I wrote about the importance of the reliability of instruments, I wondered, "What if the enemy of our souls has deployed a similar offensive counter-information attack? What if his purpose is to destroy our capability to use our compass? His weapon would be intentional offensive counter-information. *Could that entail intentional information designed to be "counter" to what we have been taught for centuries about Jesus—to get us to mistrust what we used to rely on as being fixed truth?* Would the devil go on "the air" to do it?

Think now of the phrase from Ephesians, "prince of the power *of the air*" in terms of an *on air* broadcast of information or misinformation. Is the devil smart enough to deliberately create an atmosphere by means of deliberate relentless "offensive counter-information"?

What used to be journalistic integrity has given way to a ruthless pragmatism. News anchors are now primarily media celebrities with their own "brands." Their "reporting" of the news is suspiciously similar.

I believe it was Rush Limbaugh who first began to produce what he called "montages" of the day's news coverage by the major media outlets. After listening to these compilations it became painfully clear to me that a set of talking points was released. In many cases the phrases used and even the very sequence of sentences each news anchor read was identical.

Isn't it interesting that we now call them *media outlets* rather than news broadcasts? When I hear outlet I think outlet mall—a place where stores compete for your attention to sell you something. It has been demonstrated to my satisfaction that talking points have taken the place of investigative, unbiased reporting. The facts don't matter. The optics and the impression the news teams have crafted are all that counts.

Many of these celebrity talking heads are former political consultants. Bob Beckel who ran Walter Mondale's presidential campaign recently appeared on a John Stossel special with Ed Rollins, who ran Ronald Reagan's campaign. Karl Rove, "The architect" of George W. Bush's campaigns also appeared.

The show was alternately fascinating and depressing. It was a behind the scenes exposé of what really goes on at crucial moments in political campaigns. They frankly discussed how campaign events that seemed "spontaneous" were in fact scripted parts of a clearly defined narrative crafted by paid professionals—experts in manipulating public opinion.

After the elections are over, many of these professionals are rewarded with celebrity status and proudly admit that they knew they were often promoting and defending known lies. When confronted with the intentional deception and the manipulative nature of it all, they always come back to the same rationale. "It works." A carefully constructed narrative, irrespective of its truthfulness, can be, and regularly is, sold to us on a daily basis. That this occurs in the realm of politics does not shock me. That it now takes place in the realm of theology both shocks and saddens me. Think about it for a minute.

What comprises the content of many of the books and seminars that pastors attend? Is it not primarily training in marketing "Christian" media? We have the equivalent of Christian media outlets. A Christian academic actually said to me that he was reading a book by a member of the Jesus Seminar because, "We have to compete in the marketplace of ideas." I would simply state at this point that Jesus' words are of another order than the mere marketplace of (human) ideas.

How does this relate to our topic? Two words—*Narrative Theology.* It has its roots in postmodern thought. Listen to this line of thinking:

In the post-structuralist approach to textual analysis, the reader replaces the author as the primary subject of inquiry. This displacement is often referred to as the "destabilizing" or "decentering" of the author, though it has its greatest effect on the text itself. Without a central fixation on the author, post-structuralists examine other sources for meaning (e.g., readers, cultural norms, other literature, etc.). *These alternative sources are never authoritative, and promise no consistency.*[3] (Emphasis mine.)

In his essay "Signification and Sense," philosopher Emmanuel Levinas remarked on this new field of semantic inquiry:

"It argues that because history and culture condition the study of underlying structures, both are subject to biases and misinterpretations. A post-structuralist approach argues that to understand an object (e.g., a text) it is necessary to study both the object itself and the systems of knowledge that produced the object."[4]

One of the principal thinkers who shaped post modernism and its ultimate influence on the development of Narrative Theology is Jean-Francois

Lyotard. A French philosopher, sociologist, and literary theorist, he is well known for his articulation of postmodernism after the late 1970s and the analysis of the impact of postmodernity on the human condition. He was co-founder of the International College of Philosophy with Jacques Derrida, François Châtelet, and Gilles Deleuze.

> Lyotard studied philosophy at the Sorbonne. His master's thesis, *Indifference as an Ethical Concept*, analyzed forms of indifference and detachment in Zen Buddhism, Stoicism, Taoism, and Epicureanism.[5]

Lyotard was an avowed socialist whose involvement with the first wildcat strike in France almost brought down the government. I find it fascinating that a Socialist who was a key figure in the aforementioned uprising studied Stoicism and Epicureanism—the same two schools of thought that Paul confronted at Mars Hill in Acts 17. Narrative Theology owes some of its philosophical underpinnings to a man having some (albeit remote) ties to ancient philosophies that Paul showed to be fallacious. Think back to what I said about the devil being a master tactician.

Narrative Theology which keys off postmodernism has a definite emphasis on incredulity, which is to say that there is an inherent mistrust of the existence of one story or narrative that explains everything.

It is not surprising then, that Narrative Theology leaves one with more questions than answers. I believe that labeling the revelation of God as a narrative is taking license in such a way as to possibly incur the wrath of the God whose Word is being co-opted by literary technicians.

Narrative Theology owes its shift from relying on one author's intended meaning to many meanings to writers like Roland Barthes.

> In 1967, Barthes published "The Death of the Author." Barthes argued that any literary text has multiple meanings, and that the author was not the prime source of the work's semantic content. The "Death of the Author," Barthes maintained, was the "Birth of the Reader" as the source of the proliferation of meanings of the text.[6]

Narrative Theology has taken hold in some heretofore unlikely places, like Fuller Seminary. Listen to this remark by J. R. Daniel Kirk, a Fuller faculty member. In an interview that appeared in a blog called "Narrative Theology and Transformed Meaning," Dr. Kirk wrote:

There doesn't seem to be any obvious reason why Jesus had to be born of a virgin. If he hadn't been, then there would have been no New Testament "fulfillment" of Isaiah, but then nobody would have thought there should be one! I'm inclined to think "fulfillment" should be reserved for things that are more compellingly part of what God seems to have been doing....

While few today question the validity of historical-critical exegesis, many interpreters now challenge the view that a text has only one meaning, insisting that the meaning of a text depends on the questions we ask.[7]

Dr. Kirk in his own blog writes,

In practicing a narrative theology, the overarching conviction is that the revelation of God is a story: the story of the creator God, at work in Israel, to redeem and reconcile the world through the story of Jesus.

Part of what this means for me is the possibility of transformation, reconfiguration, and even leaving behind of earlier moments in the story as later scenes show us the way forward and, ultimately, the climactic saving sequence.

Instead, I propose a multiple-reading strategy. Allow the text to mean what it meant in its first context, as much as we can determine this. Do the historical critical work that sheds light on why, for example, an eighth century BC audience would formulate matters just so—and then recognize the freedom of later readers to reread those texts differently in light of later events.... What I propose for reading the Bible itself also pertains to reading it for our communities. We are part of a long story. This means that the retellings will involve some measure of transformation. And this is, itself, faithful and living re-narration of the story of God.

This I would offer is dramatically different than the systematic theology that used to be a staple in most evangelical seminaries.[8]

Quoting the author of *Cultural Software a Theory of Ideology,* J.M. Balkin, Kirk amplifies his line of reasoning:

"Usually the characters in a narrative have reasons for what they do, and their actions have goals. The narrative either assumes or directly ascribes purposes, beliefs, and intentions to the characters."

(Note the wording here..."either assumes or directly ascribes.")

We attempt to understand what is happening in terms of expectations we already possess. We recognize patterns of behavior as meaningful in terms of patterns we are already familiar with. *We create a story about what is happening based on stock stories—expected sequences of events—that already lie to hand.* Second, the expectations that frame our understanding create the possibility of deviations from what is expected. These deviations call for explanation, and we employ stories to explain them.

(Once again, take note that the subject of all these sentences is not God, but "we." Note also the notion of "stock stories" which hearkens back to the whole area of "form criticism.")
Balkin adds,

Yet narrative is not only a framework for making behavior meaningful; it is also a framework for understanding the psychology of others and attributing mental states to them. Narrative structures organize our use of psychological concepts like purpose, desire, intention, and belief. When we explain people's behavior through narratives, we simultaneously ascribe purposes, desires, intentions, and beliefs to them.[9]

Again, it is *we* who ascribe the meaning. The meaning is not self-evident. This passage from Balkin's *Cultural Software* describes in greater detail the implications of all this:

Like other forms of cultural software, new stories are created from older ones through bricolage. Parts of stories or scripts may be combined or grafted onto each other to form new ones.

As a result, many of the stories and scripts that we possess bear structural resemblances to one another, even if they are used for widely different purposes. In the same way, we should also expect that many narratives and scripts widely dispersed in the larger culture will be strikingly similar, because they are common descendants of older stories and scripts that have been adapted to new ends.[10]

Who then, I ask, is deemed qualified to take a scissors and paste approach to what purports to be the words of the living God? What adaptations are acceptable? What criteria beyond self-appointment and literary/critical training give some the right to be the very arbiters of God's Revelation? To what ends might the stories they craft be manipulated?

Dr. Balkin makes the important observation that some will have no qualms about constructing a narrative for political and legal purposes:

Political and legal rhetoric gains much of its power from these features of narrative framing. People naturally attempt to explain gaps in events for which they have no direct evidence, or events that they do not wholly understand, in terms of familiar stories and scripts. *Once they have settled upon a story to frame events, it can exer-*

cise great power over their imagination, leading them to make unwarranted inferences and prejudicial judgments.

Trial lawyers have long understood the power of narrative framing. They attempt to lay out a story of how events occurred during their opening arguments in the hope that the jurors will use the story to frame the evidence they hear. Getting the jury to accept one side's story as the most plausible framework for the events of the trial is often tantamount to winning the case. That is because once a story is accepted, it is used to filter and organize all of the evidence subsequently presented. Like most people, jurors tend to discount or ignore evidence that does not fit their organizing story, and they will alter or simplify information so that it does conform.

Evidence that can be made to fit actually tends to reinforce the power of the story because it seems to confirm it, even though the same piece of evidence could also be consistent with a very different story. Because narrative framing is so powerful, lawyers faced with the other side's story realize that if they are to win the case they must offer an equally plausible counter-story that also fits most of the evidence. Often the only way to dislodge a narrative is with another narrative that also fits most of the facts but shows them in a very different light.[11] [Emphasis mine.]

The implications of all this are sobering indeed because the intentional creation of a narrative by those familiar with its power to shape ideology, and those who are willing to craft a narrative for a desired ideological purpose, is dangerous. Joseph Goebbels comes to mind. The Nazi narrative was finely-crafted and meticulously implemented over time. His doctorate was in literature. His background was in journalism. The net result of his tortured parsing of words and meticulous crafting of a suitable narrative was the extermination of millions of human beings… the majority of whom were God's chosen people. It appears the Devil is very skilled in Narrative manipulation.

The more pervasive and powerful a form of cultural software is in understanding the world, the more pervasive and powerful its potential ideological effects. Narrative thought is an excellent example of this phenomenon.

Because narratives are so central to our thinking, they create particularly compelling ideological mechanisms. Moreover, narratives produce ideological effects not only because they present a partial or misleading picture of the social world but because they are ways of intervening in the social world and of influencing the responses of others.

Narrative structures do not simply reflect the world badly; they shape the world to their own distorted lens. They are not only illusion but prophecy. It is as if one could make one's face become ugly by looking at it repeatedly through a funhouse mirror. Indeed, the optical metaphors of distortion are entirely inadequate to describe the variety of ideological effects that narrative thought can have on the social world.[12]

I have for a long time now had the sense that the culture is bending the church far more than the church is influencing the culture. Check the catalogues and course offerings at many Bible colleges and seminaries and note how many textbooks and course descriptions have to do with social sciences, psychology, statistics, and management. Then try to find old catalogues of the same institutions, and see how many of those course offerings were Bible-based and reliant upon systematic theology and Church history.

I began this chapter with the premise that Satan is a master of offensive counter-information tactics. I then discussed the roots and current face of Narrative Theology. I came across an interesting blog, which poses the question, "Is there a wedge being driven between Biblical Theology and Systematic Theology?" The author writes,

I have recently been undertaking some research in the relationship between Biblical Theology and Systematic Theology. In the light of this, I was intrigued by the following remarks which I came upon in a Christian magazine published in the UK:

"The wedge that has been consciously driven between systematic theology and biblical theology over recent decades in influential circles is starting to bear very bad fruit. Exclusive emphasis on the Bible as storytelling has combined with a trendy cultural impatience both with the past and with the very idea of systematic theology, and this has provided fertile soil *for the reception of the kind of ideas promoted by the scripture revisionists.*[13] [Emphasis mine.]

I believe that some have taken Narrative Theology to mean that we must get our "stories" straight, not by consulting scholars who teach systematic propositional truth from an inerrant Bible, but rather from the consensus of opinions of an increasingly secular religious cooperative. Remember the purpose of offensive counter-information is to render a group helpless and confused, in preparation for the main attack.

The desired product of an "old school" seminary was a minister who learned how to handle his compass. His systematic theology was meant to help him navigate the storms he was sure to face. Sadly, today it seems that the desired pastor/product for postmodern churches is a technician; preoccupied with polls and focus groups; slavishly adhering to the latest cultural phenomenon and desperate to be "relevant" at all costs.

Once we relegate Scripture to a subset of ancient literature, and then devalue it to the point of being merely one of many metanarratives, it is inevitable that its supernatural claims to authority will be lost. Has the devil's counter-information campaign succeeded?

NINE

TWO CLICKS AWAY: THE LOST ART OF VETTING

My friend and colleague…indeed my collaborator on this book project, Pastor Larry Johnson, has been a faithful minister for over thirty years. He and I attended seminary together in the late 1970s.

Larry is one of those pastors you would want to be there if your family was in a crisis. His preaching is rock-solid faithful to the text. He is filled with the Holy Spirit, and demonstrates both the fruit and the gifts of the Holy Spirit. His congregation knows that they have a pastor who has not wavered or surrendered to the world spirit of accommodation. His ability to do sound exposition and make pertinent application is second to none.

After thirty years of faithful service, Pastor Johnson ran afoul of his denomination's leadership. As is happening with increasing frequency all around the country, he was given a book to read by his divisional superintendent. Larry read it and found some huge inconsistencies between the author's position and the doctrinal positions of the denomination that Larry served.

Pastor Larry asked the superintendent, "Did you read this?" Embarrassed, but honest, the man replied, "No, I was told to give it to all the pastors by the district supervisor."

Later at a larger meeting of the district, a no-agenda meeting took place at which any concerns could be discussed. My stalwart friend plopped the book down and said, "Why are you recommending these books? Have you checked out these authors, and who mentored them, and who they cite as authorities?"

Admittedly his tone may have communicated a confrontational approach, but the meeting was, after all, to be "an open conversation."

When Pastor Johnson spoke, the so-called conversation was over. Two leaders took him aside and rebuked him for publicly challenging them like that. He said, "They seemed to infer that I was passionate but not very informed theologically and that even though they didn't agree with everything that was in the book, *they* had discernment and could 'eat the chicken and spit out the bones.'"

As it played out they were telling him in essence, "*We* have discernment. There is no need for you to vet the authors we recommend."

When I accepted a commission as an officer in the Navy, I lifted my hand and swore an oath. I also entered into a contractual agreement. Every drill weekend there would be a mandatory orientation for those members just joining the Reserves. They would report to "I" division ("I" as in Indoctrination) for the briefing entitled "Navy Rights and Responsibilities."

The purpose of the briefing was to make sure the newly-affiliated members knew exactly what their rights were, and what their responsibilities were. For instance, every member is subject to the Uniformed Code of Military Justice (UCMJ). They are in essence agreeing to abide by the military laws. The Navy for its part was committing to abide by the Constitution of the United States.

There is no room for nuance here. There is no room for someone saying, "I know that I lifted my hand, but I have a different take on what the rules mean."

As Pastor Johnson learned, the rules of his organization had changed. He had every reasonable right to believe that his leaders would be promoting material that was consistent to that denomination's written doctrinal statement, and its long, storied history as a conservative movement. He had the right to challenge them and they had the responsibility to show that the books they were promoting were theologically sound and consistent with the movement's historical position.

When was the last time you heard of a seminary professor being fired or asked to resign for teaching things that were contrary to the doctrinal statement they signed? Do they even still sign such statements at all? How about local church pastors? When was the last time you heard of a doctrinal committee pulling the credentials of a pastor who was preaching in such a way as to violate the stated doctrinal position of the denomination? Are pastors even screened at all as to their core doctrinal beliefs? What about supervisors?

Here is a hypothetical case. Let's say someone brings a book to a Bible study and passes it out to all the members. Is it fair to ask the person who brought it who the author is, and if the person has any information about what this author believes?"

A case in point is William Paul Young, the author of *The Shack*. After reading the book, I looked into his background and learned that he had written a paper a number of years prior to *The Shack* being published. In this paper he advocated a position that defended the doctrine of Universal Reconciliation. (This doctrine teaches that everyone will ultimately be saved, no one will be damned, and that even the devil will be spared.)

My research led me to a seminary professor who had written a book which refutes the theology inherent in William Paul Young's novel. I eventually met with Dr. James DeYoung whose book is titled, *Burning Down the Shack*.[1] I learned that he (Dr. DeYoung) had, years before *The Shack* was published, confronted Paul Young about this heretical stance. I highly recommend that every person who read *The Shack* get a copy of Dr. DeYoung's book. He exposes the intentions and theological beliefs of the team that produced the bestseller.[2]

Pastor Johnson had been told by his supervisors that they didn't have the time to look into each author's background. I don't accept that. Vetting is not always a lengthy process. I found the site that led me to Dr. DeYoung's contact information and an abstract of his book in about ten minutes with a Google search.

The expression I have used to describe vetting of sources in this digital age is *"two clicks away."* Often when I read a comment by a minister or an author, I will look at his website or blog if he has one. Then I scroll through the list of "favorites" which is usually on the right side of their blog page. This helps me see who they are reading, or in some cases, endorsing. Is there any place where I can learn what he or she believes? *Literally with two clicks of the mouse I usually begin to learn something substantial.*

I remember vetting a speaker who was scheduled to speak to a plenary session of our denomination's convention. On this person's webpage was ample evidence that he was regularly appearing at conferences hosted by Emergent Church leaders. For instance, he highly recommended reading *Love Wins*, a controversial book in which Emergent author Rob Bell challenges the biblical teaching about Hell.

In his blog the speaker I vetted said things that were much more provocative and controversial than the remarks chosen for the promo material which was presented to our ministers. Many of his beliefs were frankly at variance with the beliefs of our denomination. When I told a group of pastor colleagues what I saw, no one seemed all that concerned. In fact no one said anything at all.

When I told the same group about Paul Young's background and his agenda in writing *The Shack,* I once again was met with deafening silence. The message was clear. They neither had the time nor the inclination to look any deeper into the backgrounds of the authors whose books were being recommended. The notion of vetting carries with it the idea of scrutinizing and investigating.

"'To vet' was originally a horse-racing term, referring to the requirement that a horse be checked for health and soundness by a veterinarian before being allowed to race. Thus, it has taken the general meaning "to check."[3]

It is a figurative contraction of "veterinarian," which originated in the mid-seventeenth century. The colloquial abbreviation dates to the 1860s; the verb form of the word, meaning "to treat an animal," came a few decades later— according to *the Oxford English Dictionary,* the earliest known usage is 1891—and was applied primarily in a horse-racing context. ("He vetted the stallion before the race," "You should vet that horse before he races," etc.) By the early 1900s, vet had begun to be used as a synonym for evaluate, especially in the context of searching for flaws.

The term to "vet" also has nautical applications.

Ship/vessel vetting is the process by which a charterer determines

whether a vessel is suitable to be chartered, based on the information available to it.... Unlike certification or classification, vetting
is a private, voluntary system operators may opt to use to help them
choose a particular vessel from among all of the certified vessels
available, and to manage their risks.

Politicians are often thoroughly vetted. For example, in the United
States, a party's presidential nominee must choose a vice-presidential candidate to accompany them on the ticket. Prospective vice-
presidential candidates must undergo thorough evaluation by a
team of advisers acting on behalf of the nominee. In later stages of
the vetting process, the team will examine such items as a prospective vice-presidential candidate's finances, personal conduct, and
previous coverage in the media.[4]

Failing to vet authors and speakers and ministerial candidates can have
devastating effects in the church. In an effort to appear open-minded and
conversant with the culture, I fear many have failed to do the due diligence
necessary to ensure doctrinal soundness, resulting in the entrance of spurious
teaching to an already weakened church.

I believe that this obsession with being open-minded is the result of
decades of indoctrination by a culture that accepts as universal truth that
all faiths are right, all belief systems are equal, and the opinions of all individuals regardless of their backgrounds are to be given equal weight. This
state of affairs is, I believe, directly tied to the erosion of trust in God's Word
as being inerrant and trustworthy.

It is sobering to remember that the Bible records a period in the history
of God's people that was characterized this way:

In those days the Word of the Lord was rare, and there were not
many visions (1 Sam. 3).

Another passage shows the inevitable result of disintegration and anarchy
once we abandon the truth that God's Word is binding on all of us:

In those days Israel had no King; each man did what was right in his own eyes (Judg. 17:6).

Is this not a perfect description of the sort of anarchy and chaos we now see around the world? It really does matter whether or not we accept that God's Word is something entirely different than any other literary form. It matters when we give ourselves permission to set ourselves as redactors of His purposes. There are implications and consequences to all of this speculating and pandering to the culture.

It matters because according to God's own words to us, His revelation is of an entirely different order than the musings of fatally flawed human beings. What are we to make of these warnings?

I warn everyone who hears the words of the prophecy of this book. If anyone adds anything to them God will add to him the plagues described in this scroll: And if anyone takes words away from this scroll of prophecy, [think the Jesus Seminar] God will take away from him any share in the tree of life and in the Holy City which are described in this scroll (Rev. 22:18-19 Emphasis mine.)

Be careful to obey all these regulations I am giving you, so that it may always go well with you and your children after you, because you will be doing what is good and right in the eyes of the Lord your God. The Lord will cut off before you the nations you are about to invade and dispossess. But when you have driven them out and settled in their land, and after they have been destroyed before you, be careful not to be ensnared by inquiring about their gods, saying, "How do these nations serve their gods? We will do the same...." because in worshiping their gods they do all kinds of detestable things the Lord hates. They even burn their sons and daughters in the fire as sacrifice to their gods. See to it that you do all I command you; do not add to it or take away from it (Deut. 12: 28-32 Emphasis mine.)

Deconstructionists and Emergent Church writers are fond of mocking fundamentalists by showing how absurd it would be if we tried to enforce literally every regulation in the Old Testament. They then make the point that those passages in the Old Testament were merely guidelines for that culture, and that we today are free to reinterpret what we (meaning "they") deem to be God's intention behind the regulations through the lens of our enlightened culture.

I think both Jesus and Paul make clear that there is now a New Covenant that does not relegate the Old Testament to irrelevance but rather fulfills it in the sacrifice of Jesus for the atonement of our sins. I merely ask whether or not God's warnings about tampering with His revelation found in Scripture were merely anachronistic literary forms, or did He mean exactly what He said?

I believe *it matters to Him* a great deal how we handle His Word.

TEN

FROM TIME TO TIME

When I chose the original working title for this book, *Why It Matters*, I thought a lot about Francis Schaeffer, and I was drawn back to his 1984 book entitled *The Great Evangelical Disaster*. The precision with which he described our day is stunning.

In his book Francis Schaeffer cited a *Time* magazine anniversary edition:

> *Time* magazine recently published a special sixtieth anniversary edition with the title, *The Most Amazing 60 Years*. In recalling the world into which *Time* was born, this special issue began with the words: "The atom was split. So were most marriages."

> Here two things occurring in our era are properly brought together, one, the scientific technological explosion; and two, a moral breakdown. It is not just by accident these two things happened simultaneously. There is something which lies behind both phenomena, and in recognizing this *Time* has shown amazing comprehension.[1]

Schaeffer went on to say,

> Our culture has been squandered and lost, and largely thrown away. Indeed, to call it a moral breakdown puts it mildly. Morality itself is turned on its head with every form of moral perversion being praised and glorified in the media, and in the world of entertainment. How can we make sense of this?[2]

In the main story of the special edition *Time* offers an explanation. The essay entitled *"What Really Mattered?"* suggests, "To determine what really mattered in this jumble of events seems to require a sense of something beyond the particulars. We will need," *Time* says, "to discover the idea characterizing (our) age."

Time is quite right in this. In order to make sense of these last sixty years and equally in order to understand the present and how we as Christians are to live today, we will need to understand the idea of our age—or what we might call the spirit of the times… which has transformed our culture so radically since the 1920's.

The idea, this spirit, says *Time*, is that the idea of freedom—not just freedom as an abstract ideal, or in the sense *of being free from injustice, but freedom in an absolute sense."*[3] (Emphasis mine.)

What Schaeffer said next describes exactly what happened in Germany prior to Hitler's rise to power:

If there is not a proper balance between form and freedom, then the society will move into either of two extremes. Freedom, without a proper balance and form, will lead to chaos and to the total break-down of society. Form, without a proper balance of freedom, will lead to authoritarianism, and the destruction of individual and social freedom. But note further: no society can exist in a state of chaos. And whenever chaos has reigned for even a short time, it has given birth to the imposition of arbitrary control.[4]

As I read this chilling prediction, I was struck with the realization that what he predicted, the chaos, exists now in America in 2014. Someone or something will fill the void. As Francis Schaeffer developed this thought he concluded,

When the memory of the Christian consensus which gave us free-dom within the biblical form is increasingly forgotten, a manipu-lating authoritarianism will tend to fill the vacuum. At this point the words right and left will make little difference. There are only two roads…and the results are the same. An "elite"…authoritarianism as such, will gradually force form on society so that it will not go into chaos and most people would accept it.[5]

…AND MOST PEOPLE WOULD ACCEPT IT…."

They would accept a despot just as most Germans accepted Hitler even though they despised him as the lesser of two evils. The late Sydney Harris once quipped, "Have you ever noticed that once we deem something to be a necessary evil, it becomes more and more necessary and less and less evil?" Schaeffer describes the sad state of affairs:

As evangelical, Bible believing Christians we have not done well in understanding this. The world spirit of our age rolls on and on claiming to be autonomous and crushing all that we cherish in its path. Sixty years ago could we have imagined that unborn children would be killed by the millions here in our own country? Or that we would have no freedom of speech when it comes to speaking of God and biblical truths in our public schools? Or that every form of sexual perversion would be promoted by the entertainment media? Or that marriage, raising children, and family life would be objects of attack?

Sadly we must say that very few Christians have understood the battle that we're in. Very few have taken a strong and a courageous stand against the world spirit of this age as it destroys our culture and the Christian ethos that once shaped our country.[6]

Schaeffer explained that the Enlightenment had an enormous effect on the degradation of culture and the devaluing of the authority of the Bible:

The Enlightenment was a movement of thought which began to appear in the mid-17th century and reached its most clear-cut form in the 18th century in Germany. In general it was an intellectual movement which emphasized the sufficiency of human reason and skepticism concerning the validity of the traditional authority of the past. It is instructive to note how the Enlightenment is defined in the Oxford dictionary of the Christian church:

The Enlightenment combines opposition to all supernatural religion and belief in the all-sufficiency of human reason with an ardent desire to promote the happiness of man in this life…

Most of its representatives…rejected the Christian dogma and were hostile to Catholicism as well as Protestant orthodoxy, which they regarded as powers of spiritual darkness depriving humanity of the use of its rational faculties.

Their fundamental belief in the goodness of human nature, which blinded them to the fact of sin, produced an easy optimism and absolute faith of human society once the principles of the Enlightenment reason had been recognized. The spirit of the Enlightenment penetrated deeply into German Protestantism (in the 19th century) where *it disintegrated faith in the authority of the Bible and encouraged Biblical Criticism on the one hand, and an emotional "Pietism" on the other.*[7] [Emphasis mine.]

He described the effect that German biblical criticism had in America:

In the late 19th century it was these ideas which began to radically transform Christianity in America. This started especially with the acceptance of the higher critical methods that have been developed in Germany. Using these methods, the new liberal theologians completely undercut the authority of Scripture. We can be thankful for those who argued strenuously against the new methods and in defense of the full inspiration and inerrancy of Scripture. One would remember especially the great Princeton theologians A. A. Hodge and B.B. Warfield and later J. Gresham Machen.

But in spite of the efforts of these men and scores of other

Bible believing Christian leaders, and in spite of the fact that the vast majority of lay Christians were truly Bible-believing, those holding the liberal ideas of the Enlightenment and the destructive methods of biblical criticism came into power and control in the denominations. By the 1930s liberalism had swept through most of the denominations and the battle was all but lost.[8]

Schaeffer concluded,

It is interesting to note that there was a span of approximately 80 years from the time when the higher critical methods originated and became widely accepted in Germany to the disintegration of the German culture and the rise of totalitarianism under Hitler.[9]

How long, I have wondered, do we have before the same sort of collapse happens here? The great Evangelical disaster that Francis Schaeffer warned about is described this way:

Here is the great evangelical disaster—the failure of the evangelical world to stand for truth as truth. There is only one word for this—namely accommodation: the evangelical church has accommodated to the world spirit of the age. First there has been accommodation on Scripture, so that many who call themselves evangelicals hold a weakened view of the Bible and no longer affirm the truth of all that the Bible teaches—truth not only in religious matters, but in areas of science and history and morality.

As part of this, many evangelicals are now accepting the higher critical methods in the study of the Bible. Remember, it was these same methods which destroyed the authority of the Bible for the Protestant church in Germany in the last century, and which have destroyed the Bible for the liberal in our own country from the beginning of the century. And second, there has been accommodation on the issues, with no clear stand being taking even on matters of life and death.[10]

Interestingly, it was another *Time* Magazine cover that helped me decide on a title for my book. It was also an anniversary issue that asks the question "Does it Still Matter?"[11] The cover shows the first page of The US Constitution going through a paper shredder. I thought as I saw it that we could pose the same question about an inerrant Bible in the current "conversation" of the Emergent Church.

Martin Luther once said,

> If I profess with the loudest voice and the clearest exposition every portion of the truth of God except precisely that little point which the world and the devil are at that moment attacking... I am not confessing Christ...however boldly I may be professing Christianity. Where the battle rages the loyalty of the soldier is proved...and to be steady on all the battlefields beside is mere flight and disgrace to him if he flinches at that one point.[12]

Some, I am sure, would say, "It doesn't matter what people do or how they live. We need to honor diversity, so quit talking about moral issues." I would counter that to follow Christ is costly at just those points where the world wants us, the Church, to be silent.

I am uncomfortable likening the current climate in America to the climate in Germany during the rise of Adolf Hitler, but the parallels are inescapable. To illustrate, let's take the issue of rationing of health care and the intentional denial of care to those deemed unworthy to live due to infirmity or age.

It is well documented that the practice of eugenics involved the removal of "unfits, the eaters, the ones not worthy of life." (These are actual descriptions found in Nazi position papers written to justify murdering the mentally ill, those with Downs Syndrome, and other "incurables.")

Inge Scholl in her description of the climate in Germany went on to chronicle the sudden disappearance of mentally unfit individuals from hospitals. "Relatives would shortly learn that the individual had died, and that 'the ashes may be called for.'" Just like that.

In the current legislation that has been dubbed "Obamacare" there is actual provision for "end-of-life counseling." That is chilling. The President has himself suggested it may be time to have a "conversation" about *maybe having grandma take the pain meds instead of getting that hip replacement.*

When I brought this up in a discussion with some Christians recently I was chastised for buying into right-wing hype and not really knowing what was in the bill. Shockingly, those who challenged me did not themselves have any clue of what is being proposed. I thought of the incredible remark by the then Speaker of the House, Nancy Pelosi. She actually said, *"We will have to pass the bill to find out what is in it."*

Imagine lying in some government-run hospital, hospice, or nursing home many years from now. Imagine languishing unattended for days in soiled sheets, suffering from hunger and thirst, covered with bed sores, your flesh aboil with untreated infections. Imagine living in fear of resentful, underpaid health aides who take out their anger on you and abuse you. And imagine spending your final moments on earth in the company of a government health care worker with a syringe, who injects you with a lethal cocktail.

Do you find this hard to imagine? You should. In any civilized country, such things should not happen—ever. But President Obama's health care proposals have the very real potential to turn this nightmare into a reality for many Americans, according to an in-depth investigation reported in the August edition of *Whistleblower* magazine titled "Medical Murder: Why Obamacare could result in the early deaths of millions of baby boomers."[13]

Now when I read this, my first reaction was to pass it off as partisan talking points. Nothing like this could happen in America. I will just ask you to consider what follows, while remembering the last time you dealt with a government bureaucracy like Medicare, or Social Security, or the VA.

Especially vulnerable are the 80 million baby boomers born between 1946 and 1964. "If you belong to that group, take note," says Richard Poe, author of the August cover story. "Your generation has been targeted for a program of age-based medical rationing such as our country has never before experienced."[14]

To a small degree, Obamacare's ominous implications are starting to leak out. Here's how columnist Charlotte Allen explained it recently in the *Los Angeles Times*,

In looking for a way to fund healthcare, Obama has set his eye on the oldest and sickest. You see, according to the Centers for Medicare and Medicaid Services, about 30 percent of Medicare spending—nearly $100 billion annually—goes to care for patients during their last year of life.

What if there were no "last year of life," the president seems to be asking. Why not save billions of dollars by killing off our own unproductive oldsters and terminal patients, or—since we aren't likely to do that outright in this, the 21st century—why not simply ensure that they die faster by denying them costly medical care? The savings could then subsidize care for the younger and healthier.

And for those who have been paying close attention, Obama himself has ever-so-gently hinted at his true intentions. At a town hall event in June televised by ABC News, Obama cited the case of his grandmother, Madelyn Dunham, who died on the eve of his election, suggesting one way to cut medical costs would be to stop expensive procedures on people about to die.

"Families," Obama said, "need better information so they don't approve additional tests or additional drugs that the evidence shows is not necessarily going to improve care." "Maybe you're better off not having the surgery, but taking the painkiller," the President offered.[15]

Let me interject at this point—again in the style of Francis Schaeffer,

"Do you understand what has just been said here?" A politician, the most powerful leader on earth has just glibly offered to weigh in on whether or not your grandmother is deemed worthy of further care or consigned to an incurable status, worthy of only a maintenance pain medicine regime. And the criteria are to be set by political appointees and actuaries—done for cost savings!

Allen goes on to show that there is real reason for concern:

> Obama was slightly more explicit in a May 3 interview with the *New York Times*, when he said there ought to be a national "conversation" over whether "sort of in the aggregate," society making those decisions to give my grandmother, or everybody else's aging grandparents or parents, a hip replacement when they're terminally ill is a sustainable model. *Such decisions*, added Obama, *shouldn't be left to patients or their relatives, but to a "group" of "doctors, scientists, ethicists" who are not part of "normal political channels."*[16] [Emphasis mine.]

Notice the double-speak here? On one hand the President says, "Families need better information so that they don't approve additional tests or additional care." In another venue he leaks out his true intention. Families will not be consulted at all. A panel of unelected "experts" will decide.

Did you catch the use of the term "sustainable model"? Get used to hearing it. Progressives are fond of this sort of pragmatic, impersonal measuring stick. Think of it...a government panel determining if you or your loved one's life is sustainable.

> "One such elite medical decision-maker would be Obama's special adviser for health policy, Dr. Ezekiel Emanuel, brother of Rahm Emanuel. He's a longtime advocate of "age-weighted medical rationing"—meaning, the older you are, the less care you get, as in Britain. But what about the Hippocratic Oath, you might ask, the sacred vow doctors have always taken to do all they can to heal their patients? As *Whistleblower* documents, Emanuel advises

doctors to stop taking that oath so literally and instead to be "prudent" in assessing how much time, effort, and money each patient is worth for the greater good of society.[17]

Moreover, as "Medical Murder" reports, a bill being pushed hard by Senator Jay Rockefeller, chairman of the Senate Finance Subcommittee on Health Care, will take from Congress all authority over federal health spending and decree that such decisions in the future would be made by a secretive committee of "experts" modeled after—are you ready? – The Federal Reserve Board.[18]

At the time of this writing, I can attest to the fact that any mention of Dr. Emanuel disappeared from the "conversation" after his name became associated with the term "death panels." It was as if he never existed, that is until the Supreme Court ruled in favor of the administration—then within hours Dr. Emanuel was once again on the circuit, giving interviews that very afternoon about his progressive, sustainable, coldly logical plan for "panels." [Emphasis mine]

I bring this up in a discussion about the inerrancy of Scripture for this reason. The belief that the Bible…all of it…is God's Word to mankind, has served as a bulwark. A bulwark is a wall or embankment raised as a defensive fortification; a rampart, something serving as a defense or safeguard.

The deconstruction of the Bible and dismissal of the notion of propositional truth has a direct impact on the ethics which form the rationale for such decisions as who will live and who will be allowed to die. Conspicuously absent from Dr. Emanuel's line of thinking is any overarching moral guideline beyond the needs of the state.

Francis Schaeffer made this point time and again. The Germans justified the unthinkable because the discussion had been framed in such a way as to show that the higher good would be served by getting rid of incurables and unfits whose lives didn't serve the larger narrative. To those who think I have been too extreme by utilizing such a comparison, I report the following story which was told to me by a pastor just last week.

A man in his congregation has been battling a particularly aggressive form of cancer. The man is in his sixties. Recently the cancer has spread to his vital organs, including his liver. This family is contending in prayer for God's healing touch, however, the man had a bleeding episode and needed the ambulance. Before they left for the hospital, the ambulance driver told his wife, "Before we transport your husband, you must sign this Do Not Resuscitate order." I later learned that the man's doctor was obliged to inform him that *since he was deemed to be terminal* there was a limit on the number of units of blood he could give him.

As I previously mentioned, I submitted an op-ed piece for the *Eugene Register Guard* in which I pointed out that the current controversy surrounding Sandra Fluke and Georgetown University and the so called "War on Women" was really staged, not by an innocent coed trying to right a wrong. Rather it was the planned demonstration of an activist who was rewarded with notoriety and invitation to address the Democratic Convention. The narrative called for a trumped up "War on Women" to deflect attention away from the real reason—a cover for the abortion industry and the marginalization of the Catholic Church.

Here is the letter I wrote (which never was printed):

I am not a Catholic. I'm a Protestant minister. Catholic bashing and the attempt to drive a wedge between the church and its followers compel me to write. The recent Georgetown University stunt involving Sandra Fluke is part of a narrative contrived by progressives whose agenda is not immediately evident.

It has been open season on all things Catholic for quite a while now. Watch the video of Nicki Minaj at the 2012 Grammy Awards (she blatantly mocked the Pope) and you get some sense of how much duplicity exists in the liberal press. They called it "edgy" and "controversial." How about calling it" blasphemous" and "offensive"? Would they for a minute tolerate a performance which featured gyrating scantily-clad dancers mocking Islam? No, but this Catholic bashing serves the narrative.

Bill Maher calls females names that would make a sailor blush. He also contributes a million dollars to the progressives' candidate for president, and nary a word is said about it. Serial adulterers are given a pass by the left while their partners are labeled "bimbos" and worse. Sarah Palin would be completely justified in slapping Maher's face for what he said about her, but he's "just a comedian."

Margaret Sanger, noted proponent of eugenics and the sterilization of "unfits" is the founder of Planned Parenthood. In an interview with Mike Wallace, she was reported as saying, *"It's not only wrong, it should be made illegal for any religious group to prohibit the dissemination of birth control even among its own members." In the same interview she lauds a sexologist who was "able to clarify the question of sex and the smudginess connected with it from the beginning of Christianity."*

The Register Guard recently printed an article by Faheem Younus entitled, "Religion, Politics are best unmixed." Conspicuously absent from his article (which names only Republican offenders) is any mention of a President who is an equal offender (following the author's own logic). Remember the prayer breakfast when President Obama lectured the attendees by actually saying that Jesus would tax the rich? Okay, let's use the President's example. Jesus did talk about taxes. "Render unto Caesar (the President must like this part) the things that are Caesar's." He deftly ignores the rest of the verse."… and [render] unto God the things that are God's."

I have a friend who conducted a wolf study in the Northwest Territories. Alone in the wilderness one night, he heard horrible animal screams (think dogfight) just outside the light of his campfire. His weapon at the ready, he turned to the sound of screams. Suddenly he "just knew" to suddenly turn the opposite direction. He saw a wolf coming to get him. The pack created a diversion while the real attacker was about to take him out. The squeals from the left belie a clever attempt to focus on an invented "war on women" while the lone wolf in the form of a ravenous federal juggernaut is poised to remove the Church from any say in the matter of birth control and abortion.

We accept the nastiness of it all. Each slur, each vulgar joke left unchallenged leaves deadened nerves in the body politic. Benumbed, we have grown accustomed to it. The late Sidney Harris once quipped. "Have you ever noticed that once we deem something to be a necessary evil, it becomes more and more necessary and less and less evil?"

G. K. Chesterton captured the arrogance of those who want to police our lives to the dangerous point of forcing the narrative on the rest of us and silencing dissent, "Eugenics asserts that all men must be so stupid that they cannot manage their own affairs; and also so clever that they can manage each other's."

The point can be made that Catholic hospitals and universities are, in no small measure, responsible for the high standard of health care we all enjoy. They are within their rights to be dogmatic when it comes to Church teaching. This right comes not from the state but from God. I stand with my brethren. I stand for life.[19]

Note what Margaret Sanger said, and then factor in the fact that she was actively involved in the eugenics movement, calling for forced sterilizations, and government-mandated birth control and abortion. The same line of thinking that she espoused informed the Third Reich planners as they implemented a program of systematic murder. The citizenry, unwilling to believe that it was actually happening, just turned a blind eye.

The following appears in *Concerned Women for America*'s website. The article by Tanya L. Green is entitled "The Negro Project: Margaret Sanger's Eugenic Plan for Black Americans." Green quotes Sanger:

The most serious charge that can be brought against modern "benevolence" is that it encourages the perpetuation of defectives, delinquents and dependents. These are the most dangerous elements in the world community, the most devastating curse on human progress and expression.[20]

The *Review* printed an excerpt of an address Sanger gave in 1926. In it she said:

It now remains for the U.S. government to set a sensible example to the world by offering a bonus or yearly pension to all obviously unfit parents who allow themselves to be sterilized by harmless and scientific means. In this way the moron and the diseased would have no posterity to inherit their unhappy condition. The number of the feeble-minded would decrease and a heavy burden would be lifted from the shoulders of the fit.[21]

Sanger described the benefit of offering a bonus to those willing to be sterilized by the government:

Sanger said a "bonus" would be "wise and profitable" and "the salvation of American civilization." She presented her ideas to Mr. C. Harold Smith (of the *New York Evening World*) on "the welfare committee" in New York City. She said, "People must be helped to help themselves. Any plan or program that would make them dependent upon doles and charities is 'paternalistic' and would not be 'of any permanent value.' She included an essay (what she called a "program of public welfare,") entitled "We Must Breed a Race of Thoroughbreds."

In it she argued that birth control clinics, or bureaus, should be established "in which men and women will be taught the science of parenthood and the science of breeding." For this was the way "to breed out of the race the scourges of transmissible disease, mental defect, poverty, lawlessness, crime … since these classes would be decreasing in number instead of "BREEDING LIKE WEEDS."[22] [Emphasis mine.]

Some brave ministers still dare to speak out:

"Abortion is the number-one killer of blacks in America," says Rev. Hunter of LEARN. "We're losing our people at the rate of 1,452 a day. That's just pure genocide. There's no other word for it.

(Sanger's) influence and the whole mindset that Planned Parenthood has brought into the black community... say it's okay to destroy your people. We bought into the lie; we bought into the propaganda.

"We're destroying the destiny and purpose of others who should be here," Hunter laments. "Who knows the musicians we've lost? Who knows the great leaders the black community has really lost? Who knows what great minds of economic power people have lost? What great teachers?" He recites an old African proverb: "No one knows whose womb holds the chief."

Hunter has personally observed the vestiges of Planned Parenthood's eugenic past in the black community today. "When I travel around the country...I can only think of one abortion clinic (I've seen) in a predominantly white neighborhood. The majority of clinics are in black neighborhoods."[23]

I now know that when I say that some of the conditions that existed in Nazi German are evident in America today, it is no longer accurate to say "It *could* happen here." It *is* happening here.

The Nazi government-sanctioned murder of unfits and the destruction of any moral fiber in Germany led Sophie Scholl and Hans Scholl—the leaders of The White Rose, a courageous band of young people who opposed the third Reich—to try and do something. They began by speaking out. I too want to speak out to seminary deans, and denominational officials, and pastors in The United Sates. I want to say that no one thinks much about a bulwark until it fails.

C.S Lewis once said, "No man *suddenly* becomes base." I hold that no nation does either, nor a church, or any Christian institution for that matter. Has it mattered that we have jettisoned our trust in an inerrant Bible? Has our culture become better or worse? Is the value of human life esteemed or diminished?

I thought, as I went through this whole experience with the Eugene newspaper, of a remark by Inge Scholl. In describing the day-to-day experience of The White Rose participants, she shows how all sense of proportion was lost and that which would seem horrid in better days became strangely matter-of-fact.

> The newspapers could not report the conversation which took place at a health resort between a friend of my father's and a prison chaplain who is recuperating from a nervous breakdown. Every day he had to escort seven condemned men to the gallows.[24]

Hans and Sophie Scholl faced a choice not unlike the choice that pastors face in our day. Will we speak up and base our response to the pressing issues of our day on a trustworthy changeless Bible? Or will we, like sheep being led to the slaughter, keep quiet as our culture becomes more and more hostile to the things of God?

Will American clergy soon be defending the rationing of care for old people? Will there be clergy representation on so called ethics panels that decide who will and will not receive care? Will the same compromised clerics who "christened the ground of an abortion mill" be appointed to federal commissions in order to facilitate a "conversation" about whether or not Grandma gets the hip replacement?

The young heroes of The White Rose have given us a powerful example of what individual courage can accomplish. Inge Scholl concludes, "Perhaps genuine heroism lies in deciding stubbornly to defend the everyday things, the trivial and the immediate, after being bombarded with so much oratory."[25]

On the night before she was executed, Sophie Scholl fell asleep. She told her cell mates that she had a dream:

> It was a sunny day. I was carrying a child who was wearing a white dress in which to be baptized. The way to church led up a steep slope, but I held the child in my arms firmly and without faltering. Then suddenly the footing gave way and there was a great crevice and glacier. I had just time enough to set the child down on the

FROM TIME TO TIME

other side before plunging into the abyss. The child is our idea (she confided to her cell mate). In spite of all obstacles it will prevail.[26]

I have become convinced that sowing seeds of doubt as to the Bible's authority and trustworthiness will ultimately result in an increased vulnerability to surrender to the world spirit on the part of the masses of the people. I agree with Francis Schaeffer who predicted that in such a chaotic period, people would actually accept some form of authoritarianism as an alternative to the turmoil of such an environment.

Preachers, professors, and denominational executives have a grave responsibility in times like these. Will we hold fast to the faith that was delivered to us? Or will we succumb to the spirit of the age and blend in with the pagan environment in which we find ourselves? The jury is still out...

...and it still matters.

ELEVEN

THE CHURCH MUST SPEAK OUT

What happens when we lose our confidence in the Bible? What happens when a satanic narrative succeeds in compromising the witness of the church?

One of the most gripping images of World War II was captured in the grainy film footage which showed seemingly dazed German civilians being forced to bury the emaciated corpses of the Jews killed in the Nazi death camps. (I was stunned by a typo that occurred at this point. When I used character recognition software to dictate this paragraph, "NAZI" was typed as "NOT SEE.")

To a person, these seemingly quiet, *normal* Germans claimed to have had no knowledge whatever of the horrors that were taking place within city blocks of their homes. In the final days of the "Not see" regime, a group of incredibly brave students in Munich formed an organization I referred to previously called *The White Rose*. Two of these brave young people were a brother and sister named *Hans and Sophie Scholl*.

In 1942 Hans Scholl, a medical student at the University of Munich, his sister Sophie, Christopher Probst, Willi Graf, and Alexander Schmorell founded the "White Rose" movement, one of the few German groups that spoke out against Nazi genocidal policies.

> Nazi tyranny and the apathy of German citizens in the face of the regime's "abominable crimes" outraged idealistic "White Rose" members. Many of them had heard about the mass murder of Polish Jews. As a soldier on the eastern front, Hans Scholl had also seen firsthand the mistreatment of Jewish forced laborers and heard of the deportation of large numbers of Poles to concentration camps.[1]

After printing and disseminating leaflets to arouse the conscience of the German populace, Hans and Sophie were arrested by the Gestapo. After torture and interrogation and a show trial, they were quickly condemned to death by guillotine. Inge Scholl, their sister, later wrote a book chronicling the heroic exploits of the student resistance movement. Her descriptions of the times leading up the Nazi takeover of Germany is very telling:

> Millions of "good" Germans did not like the Nazis yet thought that they were the lesser evil compared with the communists. These "good" middle-class Germans persuaded by 1933 of the threat of communism voted for Hitler.[2]

People tend to forget that Adolf Hitler was elected. From the industrialists greedy for gain to the misguided military, too willing to obey a leader that they did not believe in, the Germans voted for Adolf Hitler. His evil philosophy was readily available in his biography *Mein Kampf.* His rabid hatred of Jews and even some hints as to how he intended to deal with them were in that book. *He simply was not vetted because he "appeared" to be what the people "thought" they wanted.*

Sophie Scholl's father compared Hitler to the Pied Piper of Hamlin, who with his flute led the children to destruction.[3] The Scholl family regularly discussed the political situation. Herr Scholl was himself a public official who eventually was arrested for a remark he made about the Führer.

Inge Scholl describes the atmosphere:

> In those days we heard a story about a young teacher who had unaccountably disappeared. He had been ordered to stand before an S.A. squad, and each man was ordered to pass by and spit in his face. After that incident no one ever saw him again. His crime? He refused to become a Nazi.[4]

Herr Scholl had taught his children well. He warned them:

"In a time of great troubles" explained father, "all sorts come to the

140

surface. Just recall the bad times we had to live through: first the war, then the difficult postwar years, inflation and great poverty… then came unemployment. If a man's bare existence is undermined, and his future is nothing but a gray impenetrable wall, he will listen to promises and temptations and not ask who offers them."[5]

The clergy were not immune to such pressures and many of them simply acquiesced to the demands of their tyrannical leaders. The spectacle of ministers in their clerical robes giving the Nazi salute is a chilling sight.

Intellectuals who opposed the Reich disappeared. Musicians, artists, and students also were rounded up if they dared to express an individual opinion contrary to the will of the Fuehrer. Those who dared to speak out, members of *The White Rose*, were heroic in every sense of that word, for they risked their lives, and many paid the ultimate price for conscience's sake.

Perhaps most striking of all is the fact that these young people had themselves been reared up as Nazis in the Hitler Youth. Both of the Scholls had been indoctrinated and exposed for years to the systematic numbing of their senses to even basic morality. Inge Scholl describes the courage it took for them to rise up against an entire nation bedeviled by evil incarnate:

We cannot take arms against the internal enemy who torments and conquers us. For us there is but one weapon: strong, tenacious and firm steadfastness. Become strong! Remain unshaken! Now we can see clearly and learned quite explicitly what lies at the bottom of the new teaching to which we have been forced to listen all these years and for the sake of which religious instruction has been banned from the schools, which has suppressed our organizations, and is now about to destroy the nursery school. It amounts to a deep running hatred of Christianity which is about to be rooted out.[6] (Take particular note of the phrase "a deep-running hatred of Christianity which is about to be rooted out.")

I don't presume to liken the current political leaders in the United States to Nazis. I do, however, make mention of the fact that the current political climate in America is rapidly becoming "anti-Christian."

The current debate about government-run health care has delved into ethical issues that border on the dangerous. So called "partial birth abortion" has been endorsed by the President of the United States. Federal money is now being allocated to organizations that provide abortion on demand. Christian organizations will be forced to offer birth control and even what has been dubbed the "just in case" pill, even though the mandate violates their religious beliefs. Wheaton University recently lost an appeal that challenged the federal government's right to do this.

The 2012 Democratic Convention featured a speech by Sandra Fluke…an activist who challenged the Catholic Institution, Georgetown University, over its refusal to pay for her birth control. *Focus on the Family* founder James Dobson (who also served on a federal commission that examined the destructive effects of pornography) recently said "Enough is enough."

Explaining that the new health care program rammed through Congress will mandate all citizens' tax money (including those who oppose it on religious grounds) to fund abortions, he actually said in a nationally aired radio interview on the Sean Hannity show, "Come and get me Mr. President."[7] The saddest part to me is the fact that I know ministers who have openly ridiculed Dobson for his strident opposition to federally-funded abortions.

Military chaplains are now warned against praying in Jesus' name, yet encouraged to find ways to be creative on navigating the "new normal" of same-sex couples in their chapels. What about the clergy of today, are they/we in danger of simply going along with the current culture? Are we reduced to lifting a moistened finger to the wind, altering our doctrine to suit the culture, or worse, surrendering to what we know to be evil?

The current Emergent Church *conversation* is quick to point out that the "religious right" has erred in getting too political while the leaders of the Emergent Church have no qualms with getting in bed with left-leaning radicals, all in the name of creating community.

Jonathan Merritt in his 2012 book titled, *A Faith of Our Own—Fol-*

lowing Jesus Beyond the Culture Wars, bases much of what he says on polls, like this one:

> The church is hemorrhaging from the inside. As Christian involvement in the culture wars swelled over the last several decades, regular church attendance slouched— interrupted briefly during the months following the 9/11 attacks. Why are they leaving? According to a Gallup poll, when Americans were asked to explain the decline in religious observance that they were seeing around them, one of the most frequent replies was the church was too involved with current social and political battles.[8]

He goes on to condemn the current tone in political discourse:

> Christians need a rapid infusion of what Peggy Noonan calls "patriotic grace," which is to say, "a grace that takes the long view, apprehends the moment wherein, comes up with ways of dealing with it, and eschews the politically cheap and manipulative." Many of the folks I've spoken with want exactly that. They desire what John Murray Cuddihy called a "culture of civility". They long for the day when the American public square will be a place of passionate and reasonable discussion resembling the Greek Agora more than the Roman Coliseum.[9]

I have to say that for all the calls for civility, one side seems to have a pattern of making outlandish hateful remarks. Then with prepared apologies in hand, it immediately prepares for the next round with even more egregious attacks and prepared apologies and so it goes.

One thought seems to repeatedly come out in the "conversation" though, "Christians need to be silent about the so called "culture wars" issues—cases in point—gay rights and abortion. Even the term "culture wars" is probably the result of talking points created to silence the so called "religious right."

Merritt's book reflects a bias that it is the Christians who need to adapt, and that the poll he quotes makes a huge assumption that declining numbers in church attendance are the direct result of Christian involvement in politics. I would offer that there is another completely plausible explanation for the decline in attendance. It may well be that we are living in the Last Days, and that a falling away that was prophesied in the Bible is taking place. It can also be that people are leaving churches because of liberal neglect of biblical preaching.

I have personally interviewed fellow pastors who actually physically squirmed in their chairs as they talked about how to "approach the issue" of abortion on demand. Wringing their hands, they seem legitimately perplexed.

When it comes to same-sex marriage or the topic of homosexual behavior in general, many give a look that seems to say, "Don't even go there." I described the actual procedure known as late-term abortion at a pastors' gathering. Many looked at me as if I was some sort of ghoul for merely describing what actually takes place to a real living baby at the hands of a government funded "health care" professional.

Jonathan Merritt (whose father was once the president of the Southern Baptist Convention) urges Christians not to focus on just a few issues, coincidentally—abortion and gay marriage. What about poverty? What about saving the planet? What about social justice? He cites two Emergent Church notables:

> Authors Shane Clairborne and Jonathan Wilson-Heartgrove witnessed similar divisions when engaging the issue of poverty. They noted that the church, which should be unified in its love for and support of the poor, has been held captive by the world's debates over the issue.

> Christians on the right argued that the best way to reduce poverty was to encourage capitalistic growth through tax breaks while Christians on the left countered that we needed more taxes for government programs that assist people's basic needs and work to alleviate the causes of poverty.

"We're not sure who is right, but we have noticed that the debates don't seem to do much for the people in our neighborhoods."

Clairborne and Wilson-Heartgrove write:

What it does unfortunately is to divide the church... Rather than share what we have in common so that no one has need, we self-aggregate into conservative and liberal congregations or black and white congregations or upper and lower class congregations.[10]

Again the noble rhetoric about poverty avoids and deflects a frank discussion about what the Word of God has to say about abortion and gay marriage. Here is why I think this occurs. A detailed discussion about poverty will not cause offense. Becoming an activist against the proliferation of nuclear weapons will not result in one being labeled as a controversial "culture wars" combatant, for this issue aligns with the current progressive narrative, and does not require identification as a person who believes that the Bible speaks with authority about the "other" issues.

Citing yet another poll, Merritt says:

Today about 42 percent of Americans call themselves "pro-choice" and 51 percent call themselves pro-life. We've reached an ideological stalemate, and many of today's *Christians have tired of the debate.* The sound bites are worn out, the rhetoric is often devoid of basic civility, [there's that call for civility again... how civil can one be in talking to another who believes that infanticide is somehow justifiable?], and despite the best Christian efforts we've failed to induce much movement on the issue in the last 30 years. Americans are tired of the rancor and name calling.[11] [Emphasis mine.]

I thought about Dan Merchant at this point. His documentary *Lord Save Us from Your Followers* is filled with clips in which he tells us all what "most" Americans think. I know as many Americans who feel just as strongly that the church has failed to make her voice heard on both these issues. They also feel that these are not some sort of "side issues." Clearly they are not side issues to our Lord. Merritt goes on,

> "It has not only become non-productive but it has almost become boring. People are not weary of the cause, but they are tired of the debate itself," says Joel Hunter, the pro-life pastor of Northland Church. "Since overturning Roe v. Wade isn't realistic in the fore-seeable future, if you're pro-life you have to find different ways to combat abortion. I have always been a person that thinks that employing many methods is more effective than one method. Any progress we can make is still progress." Progress for Hunter involves using our collective resources to reduce the impetus for abortion in America.[12]

Listen to this subtle shift away from addressing the stark reality of abortion and the legitimate immediate crisis facing ministers who believe their Bibles. We are confronting wanton murder, and are now reduced to conceding that the debate is over and looking for ways to perhaps stave off the need for future abortions. I am not questioning Pastor Hunter's intentions. I am, however, suggesting that his urging the church to back off on confronting this issue may be being used by others whose agenda is much more pointed.

Merritt's pastor, Joel Hunter, also commented on the "image problem" that the religious right has given the church:

> As I've observed young Christians and considered my own changing perspective in recent years, there seem to be several reasons why the movement is heading in a new direction. No one will deny that there is a reaction against the past several decades of Christian political engagement. They're embarrassed by the way our faith has been represented to a watching world as little more than a political movement.

> "It is like our crazy Uncle Harry got out of the home and ran into

City Hall wearing a shirt with the family name," comments Joel Hunter. "We love him, but he misrepresents us.'" [Emphasis mine.]

Merritt asks, "Who is right?"

To some extent, both are. They each picked up on important biblical scenes, but they've done so at the exclusion of others. The Bible has become more manageable in both cases, but it has been robbed of its magnitude and Majesty, which rests on its being embraced as a whole.[13]

I ask at this point, who determines what the whole Bible is? Who determines what is authentic, and what is the product of redactors and faith communities? Are the passages that condemn homosexuality inspired or merely anachronistic culturally driven mores that are irrelevant now? Is there any consequence to the wholesale slaughter of innocents that we as a nation countenance?

Merritt shows that he doesn't have much regard for backward types who believe that the Bible is prescriptive and that there is such a thing as propositional truth:

I think about the infomercials for the late Jack LaLanne's power juicers that still run when only third-shift cashiers are watching. Imagine a pruny but strangely fit old man in a spandex body suit leaping around and declaring that the secret to long life is nothing more than fruit juice. Reaching into a silver bowl, he throws heaping handfuls of fruit and vegetables—carrots, apples, kale, bananas, into the hole atop his patented machine. The appliance gargles and grinds until it spits out a shot glass of muddy juice.

Christians have often done likewise when engaging the public square events. Evangelicals, for example, often reduce the immense witness of Scripture to only a few culture war issues, namely abortion and gay marriage. Both are important issues deserving serious thought. The Scriptures speak often about life and sexuality. But they also regularly address poverty, equality, justice, peace, and the care of God's good creation.[14]

I can almost hear the late Francis Schaeffer say, "Do you understand what has been said here?" Christians who narrow their focus to abortion and gay rights issue are "like a prunish old man peddling muddy juice." People who get aggressive in their opposition to the abortion and the gay agenda are likened to Crazy Uncle Harry—escaped from "the home."

C.S. Lewis once said, "A wrong sum can be made right…but never by merely going on." These issues—gay marriage and abortion—are troublesome to everyone. No one wants to be cast in the role of "bigot "or "hater." The answer, however, is not to just change the subject.

Christian artist Phil Keaggy said it powerfully in his song, "Who Will Speak Out for the Little Ones?"

"Who will speak out for the little ones, helpless and half abandoned… They've got a right to choose…life they don't want to lose…I've got to speak out, won't you?"

Twelve

IT COULD HAPPEN HERE

The lack of seriousness with which the students here speak of God and the world is, to say the least, surprising…over here one can hardly imagine the innocence with which people on the brink of their ministry, or someone already in it ask questions in the seminar for practical theology—for example whether one should preach of Christ. In the end with some idealism and cunning we will be finished with this—that is their sort of mood.[1]

These are the words of Dietrich Bonhoeffer, the courageous clergyman and theologian who fought Hitler and paid with his life for holding fast to the Word of God. Long before his involvement with a plot to kill Hitler, Bonhoeffer had to battle fellow Christians who had acquiesced to the Nazification of the Church. He had an acute understanding of the gravity of the situation facing Christians in Germany.

As things became more and more dangerous for him, he made one last trip to America. Friends were trying to get him a position at a seminary in New York. They knew he was a dead man if he returned to Germany. As he wrestled with whether or not to return, he languished in New York. As he observed Union Seminary and the state of the church in America, he wrote,

The theological atmosphere at Union is accelerating the process of secularization of Christianity in America. Its criticism is directed essentially against the fundamentalists…it is carried away with general collapse. A seminary in which it can come about that a large number of students laugh out loud in a public lecture at the quoting of Luther's "Sevo Arbito"…on sin and forgiveness…because it seems to them comic has evidently forgotten what Christian Theology by its very essences stands for.[2]

He cites this example of the dismissive attitude of Harry Emerson Fosdick:

> In a homiletics seminar, Fosdick gave out sermon topics. A few of them were on what he condescendingly called "traditional themes." Bonhoeffer was stunned that in this category was a sermon "on the forgiveness of sin and the cross." He said, "the heart of the gospel has been marginalized and quaintly labeled, 'traditional.'"[3]

His further comment is especially pertinent to the critique of the Emergent Church of our day:

> This is quite characteristic of the churches I saw. So what stands in the place of the Christian message? An ethical and social idealism borne by a faith in progress that—who knows here—claims the right to call itself "Christian"... And in the place of the church as the congregation of believers in Christ there stands the church as a social corporation.[4]

I find that remark fascinating in light of the current Emergent shift in emphasis away from the substitutionary atonement to a gospel of good works (i.e. eradicating poverty in our time). While apologizing for the more troublesome claims of Christ—that repentance and belief in Him is the only way to be saved—and downplaying our certainty of these essential truths, we become somehow more fashionable and much more accommodating to the culture.

Bonhoeffer's experience at Union and his subsequent battles with those who identified themselves as the "German" Christians is eerily similar to today's scene in America. Progressive notions of the superiority of man's intellect and reason are fast becoming the replacement for what used to be known as the doctrine of the depravity of the soul. Both of these things cannot be universally true. In the one instance man says that he is a being that is evolving into higher states of consciousness and is the arbiter of what is true about God and about himself. In the other, the biblical instance, man is described as being possessed of a heart that is deceitfully wicked, incapable of knowing his own heart, and bent on evil continually.

Some fair questions might be:

- Was Bonhoeffer right?
- Did his predictions come true?
- What happened then as a result of the German Church adopting such a low view of Scripture? Did it have any real world consequences?

Adolph Hitler had contempt for Christianity. Although he, like many politicians today, mouthed platitudes, and feigned allegiance to the God of the Bible, he held pastors and Christianity in extremely low regard. He once lamented,

It's been our misfortune to have the wrong religion. Why didn't we have the religion of the Japanese who regard sacrifice for the fatherland as the highest good? The Mohammedan religion too would have been much more compatible to us than Christianity. Why did it have to be Christianity with its meekness and flabbiness?[5]

Eric Metaxas in his book on Bonhoeffer described a plan to turn the existing German churches into Nazi churches:

How they would get there was a point of some disagreement. Some, like Himmler wanted to start fresh, while others thought it easier to turn the existing churches into Nazi churches over time. Rosenberg was "an outspoken Pagan" who during the war developed a thirty point program for the "National Reich church." That it was entrusted to an "outspoken pagan" shows how much respect Hitler had for the Christian church and its doctrines. Rosenberg's plan is some of the clearest proof of the ultimate plans for the churches.

Here are a few of the things they had in store:

- Point 13—The National Church demands immediate cessation of the publishing and dissemination of the Bible in Germany.
- Point 15—The National Church will clear away from its altars all crucifixes and pictures of the saints.
- Point 19—On the altar must be nothing except a copy of *Mein Kampf* (…to the German nation and therefore to God the most sacred book) and to the left of it a sword.
- Point 30—On the day of its foundation, the Christian cross must be removed from all the churches, cathedrals and chapels…and it must be superseded by the only unconquerable symbol—the swastika.[6]

Clearly it mattered to the Nazis that there existed a Book that claimed to be the inerrant Word of God. When it didn't work to try and blend the two versions of the church, the German Christians changed tactics. Mataxas writes:

As they bent themselves into pretzels, some German Christians realized that it was a losing battle. So in 1937 a group of them stated that the written Word of Scripture was the problem. Whereas the Jews were the first to write out their faith, they said Jesus never did so. "True German Christianity" must therefore move beyond written words.[7]

How similar that line of logic is to today's Emergent tortured parsing of the meanings of what are deemed to be "problematic" assertions of the unique claims of Christ and his definitive judgment on certain behaviors. So-called Narrative Theology is a construct tailor-made for just such an attempt to downplay the Scriptures that get in the way of affirming postmodern notions of uncertainty and ambiguity.

It is as though some postmodern preachers are saying, "I know it is written to sound a certain way, but the larger narrative, the story, is meant to convey a truth that is much more palatable to a postmodern reader or listener. So don't say, "The Bible says,…" rather, "tell the story" about Jesus and how nice He was and all the good things He did.

The Nazis understood that it was essential to remove any vestiges of biblical truth. They so feared the Bible that even the hint of it sent the Gestapo scurrying to stamp it out:

> One Nazi leader sent the Gestapo a letter complaining that the melody to the hymn "Jerusalem Thou City High and Fair" was played at memorial services for the German war dead. There were no offensive words, since only the melody was played but even to evoke the memory of the words was unacceptable.[8]

Hitler saved some of most vicious words for the clergy. He knew how to deal with the Protestant ministers:

> "You can do what you want with them," he once remarked. "They will submit…they are insignificant little people, submissive as dogs, and they sweat with embarrassment when you talk to them. Hitler and his Reich Bishop Mueller used to refer to pastors as "Pfaffen"… a composite word made up of the words "pfarrer" (pastor) and "Affen" (apes).

I asked earlier, "What was the result? What consequence followed the collapse of a true Christian church in Germany?" Well, for one, the Nazis faced little or no opposition to the wholesale slaughter of those they deemed inferior:

> In 1933 the anti-gospel of Hitler was moving to the legal murder of these people who like the Jews were categorized as "unfit," as a drain on the German economy. The term increasingly used to describe those people with disabilities was "useless eater" and "life unworthy of life." When the war came in 1939, their extermination would begin in earnest.[9]

Unlike Bonhoeffer who had no illusions as to the Nazis' end game, some pastors like Martin Niemoller tried to placate or at least get along with the German Christians. They felt that somehow they could reason with Hitler. It was years later as he languished in a concentration camp that Martin Niemoller penned these famous words:

> First they came for the Socialists and I did not speak out because I was not a Socialist.
> Then they came for the trade unionists and I did not speak out because I was not a trade unionist. And then they came for the Jews and I did not speak out because I was not a Jew. And then they came for me… and there was no one left to speak for me.[10]

Dietrich Bonhoeffer knew full well the inevitable consequence of trying to compromise on things which the Bible says are non-negotiable. How well he put it,

> If you board the wrong train, it is of no use running along the corridor in the opposite direction.[11]

Before I leave the discussion of Hitler's takeover of the church, I want to say with some embarrassment that it was a (German) Navy Chaplain who helped him do it:

> "With the election of Mueller as the Reich Bishop the lines were drawn. His election was yet another stick in the eye of the confessing church." "It was," said Metaxas, "as if Gomer Pyle had become The Archbishop of Canterbury."[12]

Hellish in its symbolism, the ceremony in which Muller was consecrated Reich Bishop was held in a place that would make the point that biblical Christianity was being replaced by a church with Satanic approval:

The election of the crew-cut dullard Mueller took place at Wittenburg Castle…over Luther's tomb.[13]

The Devil it seems has a great interest in the formation and training of those who minister. Paul used the phrase "doctrines of demons." Was he speaking figuratively, or did he believe that there was a personal Devil who actually tried and continues to try to influence the doctrines of the church?

I have a little thing I do mentally that helps me gain a wider perspective. Perhaps you have seen or used Google Earth. It really is amazing. Fire up your laptop at Starbucks, sip your latte, and you can zoom in from outer space and see your driveway. What I do is to mentally do the opposite. I zoom out—way out—to the place Paul described as the heavenly places.

I used to picture our church property—zoom out—way, way out, and then imagine how our situation appeared to those looking on from that perspective. If you even have a partial belief that the Bible is God's Word, then from the perspective of Satan, the Bible colleges and seminaries would be of particular interest. Denominational headquarters and local churches would also require his attention…particularly when it came to the way in which the belief in an inerrant Bible was handled…how the conversation was framed, if you will.

An incident from my own experience got me thinking about all this. When I attended the Basic School to become a Navy Chaplain, I had an encounter that brought this issue into crystal clarity. Each morning we would, as a class, have devotions in the chapel. One or more of the students or candidates would be tasked with putting together a worship service. There were two objectives:

- We were there to begin our day in worship.
- We were being evaluated as to how we would conduct ourselves as Priests, Rabbis, and Ministers in the fleet. (We had at that time not yet commissioned the first Muslim chaplain).

When it came time for me to lead devotions, I chose two or three passages of Scripture, led a series of hymns and choruses, then preached a brief message based on the Scriptures I chose. I was so nervous I am to this day hard-pressed to tell you *what* I preached on. What I do remember though is the reaction of one of my fellow students.

After the service he came up to me and said, "I want to talk with you as soon as possible about some of what you said this morning." We agreed that as soon as we could arrange it we would talk. Three or four nights later we met at a fast food restaurant on the base.

After exchanging pleasantries he said, "I was fascinated by something you said. Do you mean to say that you actually believe in a personal devil?" After my jaw popped back from the floor, I asked him, "And do you mean to tell me that you don't?"

He went on to give me a lecture about higher criticism, and how he didn't believe in the virgin birth, the bodily resurrection of Jesus, the inerrancy of Scripture, or "any of that stuff." I truly believe the man thought he had done me a favor; helping get my head straight on things.

Two thoughts careened around in my head:

- Somewhere in the not too distant future, some ship's crew or battalion of Marines or Coast Guard detachment would have this man as their chaplain—and he didn't believe the Bible was entirely inspired and completely true.
- He and I could not be more different, and the relatively cloistered ministerial experience I had previously enjoyed was now going to change...radically.

There was another incident that took place in that same chapel. One morning a Baptist minister was leading and he, like me, quoted a handful of verses. He was reading the *King James Version*. As he preached I heard a sound behind me. "Hoomphff!" It sounded like someone was stifling a sneeze but with a great deal of anger or frustration.

I discreetly turned around to trace the source of this noise and saw a female chaplain with her arms crossed, her eyes shooting darts at the preacher. She wasn't having an asthma attack...she was angry. But what could this man have said to warrant such a response? All he was doing was quoting the Scripture.

Later I learned my female colleague took issue (and actually lodged a complaint) having to do with the chaplain using the offensive "gender specific" references in the Bible. I remembered thinking at the time (1988), *Will this sort of thing, taking issue with actual wording of the Bible, ever gain any traction? Am I overreacting?*

Twenty years later, I went into a Christian Bookstore. The young lady who was helping me find a Bible ushered me to the section where the various translations were displayed. I had asked her to find me a study Bible with extra, extra large print. What she said next caught me totally off guard.

"Okay, so before we go any further, I need to explain—a sort of disclaimer—before you look at this one. I need to tell you that there is some controversy." She then went on to show me that on this shelf there was the "old" Bible and that on this shelf was the "new" one—the one which didn't contain any offensive references to gender specificity."

In a mere twenty-year period what I once perceived as a fringe issue raised by a feminist had become mainstream enough to warrant a disclaimer. I was struck with that word *"dis... claimer"— a statement that disavows a claim.* In this instance the claim that the Bible as we have known it is really valid for our day, that it is in fact what it purports to be, the Word of God containing the "faith that was once for all delivered to the saints."

As I recalled these two troubling incidents I thought they were related. In the one instance I had a minister who had been trained to treat the Bible as mere literature, filled with principles and motifs but nothing more, certainly not literal, historical facts. This led him to conclude that the devil is an archetype, not a person.

The other chaplain had been equally shaped by her view that the Scripture was sexist (the very term "sexist" is a fairly recent addition to the lexicon). Since it was merely a compilation of primitive religious beliefs that were outdated, it was incumbent upon us to rid ourselves of such irrelevant and offensive language.

Zooming out to the realm of the "heavenlies," I ask myself, "Would it serve any Satanic agenda to create a climate in which this kind of doubt and skepticism would grow? Might the Devil be behind the push to demythologize the Bible? Could we be seeing his handiwork in the chaos surrounding any discussion to do with gender issues? Has this personal Devil, a being that existed before the creation of human beings, ever questioned the veracity and reliability of God's Word before? Is he really the Father of lies? Has he evolved or is he still a liar?"

If you believe as I do that the references to the Devil in the Bible are literal and refer to a real person, not a "motif" or a "construct" or an "archetype," then it becomes (if you accept the biblical description of the Devil, how he thinks, what he says and does, etc.) extremely plausible, probable in fact, that he would still be about the business of creating doubt and trying to get people to mistrust God. It is not in vain that he is described as a "roaring lion seeking whom he may devour" (1 Pet. 5:8, KJV).

In Genesis 3, we read the Devil's first recorded utterance to a human being, "HATH GOD TRULY SAID... ?"

Once the subject was introduced he then cast aspersions on the motives and the character of God, telling the woman that God gave prohibitions because didn't want the best for his creatures (see Gen. 3:4-5). Here we have it, a full frontal assault on the concept of truth and on its direct relationship with the very nature of God.

The early church was forced to face the whole issue of false teachers who taught doctrines that were deemed to be heretical. Substantial portions of the Early Church Fathers' writings consisted of the refutation of just such aberrant teachings. Throughout the history of the church the same challenges to the faith recur with astonishing regularity. Here is a sampling of quotes for the early Church Fathers:

- Clement of Rome, AD 90–100, wrote, Look carefully into the Scriptures which are the true utterance of the Holy Spirit. Observe that nothing of an unjust or counterfeit character is written in them. (I Clement xiv)
- Ireneaus c. 175-c.195—(We are) most properly assured that the Scriptures are indeed perfect, since they were spoken by the Word of God and His Spirit...all Scripture, which has been

given to us by God shall be found by us perfectly consistent. (Against Heresies, II, xxviii)

- Chrysostom (c. 344/354–c.407)—There is divergence in the narratives of the Gospel…but there is no contradiction.
- Augustine (354-430)—Lord, surely your Scripture I, for You being truthful and truth itself have produced it… Oh man, what my Scripture says, I say. (Confessions, XII, xxix)
- Martin Luther (1438-1546) – The Scriptures have never erred. Every Word of the Bible is God's Word and therefore the Bible is without error.
- Louis Gaussen (1790-1863. Swiss Reformed)—The ancient church viewing the whole Scripture as an utterance, on the part of God, addressed to man, and dictated by the Holy Ghost, has ever maintained that there is *nothing erroneous* [emphasis mine], nothing useless, nothing superfluous there; and that in this divine work, as in that of creation, one may always recognize amid the richest plenty the greatest and the wisest economy.
- Adolphe Monod (1802–1856, French)—The more I study the Scriptures, the example of Christ and the Apostles, and the history of my own heart, the more I am convinced that a testimony of God, placed without us and above us, exempt from all intermixture of sin and error which belong to a fallen race, and received with submission on the sole authority of God, is the true basis of faith.
- B.B. Warfield (1851–1921, American theologian)—Thus in every way possible, the church has borne her testimony from the beginning and still in our day, to her faith in the divine trustworthiness of her Scriptures.
- Harold Lindsell, (American) author of *The Battle for the Bible* – There is no evidence to show that errancy was ever a live option in the history of Christendom for eighteen hundred years in (any) branch of the Christian church that had not gone off into aberrations.[14]

Just as the testimony to an inerrant Bible is consistent, so is the lie that resurfaces from time to time. I suppose one shouldn't be surprised. The lie is the same because the liar is the same, and his tactics are recorded for anyone to see…in the Bible. C.S. Lewis remarked that the most successful ploy of the devil is to convince people that he doesn't exist.

I ask whether or not it would serve the purpose of such a being to create a maze of doubt and uncertainty just to deflect attention away from him. Get them to doubt the inerrancy of the Bible and it is really just a few steps away from treating the Bible solely as archaic literature no more inspired than any other dead religious tome.

Emergent church guru Rob Bell questioning the existence of Hell is nothing new. Leonard Sweet deconstructing the "traditional" understanding of the church in favor of quantum religion is put forth as new cutting-edge religious innovation. It can also be construed as an age-old error in a new package.

I believe that the devil is behind the whole notion of deconstructing and dissection and dissembling. Think about it. The antichrist in order to have the infrastructure to control the masses must first rid himself of all religious vestiges of loyalty to any other deity but himself.

To do his he must, over time:

- Cause the masses to first doubt the doctrines of their own faith
- Co-opt the training of their ministers
- Create an atmosphere in which tolerance trumps tenacity to doctrine.

Once there is a religious wasteland and people are jaded, the antichrist will then reveal that he is the embodiment of all the hopes of all the religions he has systematically compromised. He will then with false signs and wonders seal the deal. Again this only makes sense if you believe the Bible… all of it.

THIRTEEN

THE OFFENSE OF THE CROSS

The church stood poised between two crosses, wanting to be loyal
to both but learning that neither cross could tolerate the other. The
church made peace with an enemy with which it should have been
at war. Called to warn and protect,
It tolerated ...
Then saluted ...
Then submitted.

ERWIN LUTZER – HITLER'S CROSS

I started this book recounting an incident that took place in a relatively
obscure place in British Columbia. Thirteen years later the church in
North America has seemingly lost her anchor. At a loss to explain the
declining numbers, the church has embraced the notion that it is the message of the cross that is somehow deficient.

SACKCLOTH OR SHEEPSKINS?

Rather than repenting in sackcloth, church leaders now strive to earn sheep-
skins—in management theory, strategic leadership, cultural studies, and other
disciplines that exalt human potential. I remember reading that once-upon-
a-time theology was "the mother of all the disciplines." Today, course offerings
in classical theology are rapidly disappearing from seminary catalogues.

Francis Schaeffer, in *The Great Evangelical Disaster* related a sad story
about Bishop James Pike:

Several years ago at the Roosevelt Auditorium in Chicago, I had a
dialogue with Bishop James Pike (Bishop Pike was a leading liberal
in the Episcopal Church). Some years before our dialogue, he had

been brought to trial in the Episcopal Church on heresy charges. However the charges were eventually dropped—not because his views were in fact orthodox, but because the Episcopal denomination had accepted theological pluralism and relativism and therefore had no real basis upon which to practice discipline.[1]

Schaeffer had this to report about their dialogue:

A clear statement was raised, with a clear statement of differences, without destroying him as a human being. At the close he said, "If you ever come to California please come to visit me in Santa Barbara."

Later when Edith and I were out in Santa Barbara we went to his place and were able to carry on a further discussion with him without one iota of compromise, and yet again not destroying him, but letting him know we respected him as a human being.

We also talked about the possibility that his belief that he was talking to his son "on the other side" was really a matter of demonology. This was some time after Bishop Pike's son had committed suicide, and he had tried to communicate with his son through a medium. And he did not get angry though he was close to crying.[2]

What Schaeffer said next illustrates the passion that led me to write this book.

I will never forget the last time I saw him (Bishop Pike), as Edith and I were leaving the Center of the Study of Democratic Institutions. He said one of the saddest things I have ever heard:

"When I turned from being an agnostic, I went to Union Theological Seminary, eager for and expecting bread; but when I graduated, all that it left me was handful of pebbles."

Schaeffer asks a sobering question,

Who is responsible for the tragedy of Bishop James Pike? His liberal professors who robbed him of everything real and human.... We cannot take lightly the fact that liberal theological professors in any theological school are leaving young men and women with a handful of pebbles and nothing more....

We must do all that is necessary for the visible church to exhibit the holiness of God; and yet, no matter how bitter the liberals become or what nasty things they say or what they release to the press, we must show forth the love of God in the midst of the strongest speaking we can do.[3]

I have attempted to show that the things Schaeffer predicted in 1984 have come to pass. As I read the words of Charles Spurgeon, and Harold Lindsell, and John Warwick Montgomery, and W. A. Criswell, and John MacArthur, and others, I come away with a sense of urgency that I add my voice to theirs in calling to this generation, "To the law and to the testimony..."

In an effort to reach a culture that has long since abandoned the Bible, Christians who identify themselves as progressives have taken the wrong course. Like a sailboat tacking to the wind, they have intentionally sought to catch the winds of doctrine that Paul warned us about. Flummoxed when they fail to see the results they expect, they double down on accommodations of their own creation.

Erwin Lutzer has written an important book titled *Hitler's Cross.* In it he shows the striking parallels that exist between the behavior of the Christian Church in Germany as Hitler rose to power and the current behavior of some Christians in America today:

Popular German culture, with its myths about race and occultism, thrived in place of sound biblical teaching and prayer. The Church overlooked the fact that the fight against Nazism was essentially not political but spiritual. The church mistook the temporal benefits of the swastika for the spiritual benefits of the cross of Christ. Wanting to believe that Hitler was the answer, it forgot what the really important questions were.[4]

The results, as Lutzer powerfully illustrated, were tragic:

The church stood poised between two crosses, wanting to be loyal to both but learning that neither cross could tolerate the other. The church made peace with an enemy with which it should have been at war. Called to warn and protect, it tolerated…then saluted… then submitted. [5]

Allow me to recap what I have written. Back near the watershed, over twenty years ago in British Columbia, I stumbled on to a ceremony in which a plan to merge progressive politics and New Age spirituality was publicly announced.

Three years after that meeting a group calling itself a *Parliament of World Religions* met in Chicago:

Six thousand delegates came from all over the world to discuss the need to unite the religions of the world. The assumption was that world hunger war and injustice are so staggering that *only a unified religion and government can solve these problems.* A global ethic was adopted, in which the word God does not appear, but the word EARTH is capitalized throughout. The document says that there cannot be a transformation of earth unless there is a transformation of consciousness.[6]

This "transformation of consciousness" has been methodically introduced to our education system, our political decisions, and our spiritual lives as well. The same folks who planted the Peace Pole have continued their efforts to set the stage for something…or someone.

The Parliament of World religions put it this way:

In conclusion we appeal to all the inhabitants of the planet. Earth cannot be changed for the better unless the consciousness of individuals is changed. *We pledge to work for such transformation individual and collective consciousness, of the wakening of our spiritual powers.* Together we can move mountains."[7]

I talked about how the Emergent Church "conversation" has political overtones, and that its political ties to a green movement are much more substantial and consequential than they initially seem.

Has any of what I saw in Canada had any real world consequences? Have some of the agenda items of the World Peace University Society been implemented?

After Bill Clinton left office there were stories floated for months about his possible ambitions after being President. There was speculation that the job he really wanted was Secretary General of the United Nations. His foundation began to build strategic partnerships.

He appeared on the cover of the October 1, 2012 issue of *Time* magazine:

All around the world in poor countries and rich ones, the private sector, governments and no-profits are combining their skills and resources to form networks of creative cooperation to boost local economies while addressing problems like climate change and poverty.[8]

Remember the goals of The World Peace University Society? Listen to this example in which the former president describes what is behind his foundation's initiatives:

"Smallholder farmers in Africa are planting trees so they cannot only harvest timber or fruit but also profit by selling carbon credits on the open market…"[9]

Think back to what was said in the article about the World Peace

University Society and the UN money back in 1990. Does it not sound a lot like the priorities of Maurice Strong and Al Gore? Clinton cites an example of what this fundamental change will look like:

> "If sustainable energy were bad economics, Costa Rica wouldn't be one of the richest countries in the region with what is arguably the greenest economy in the world."[10]

What he fails to mention is that there is a huge amount of UN money underwriting all this green "success." Remember Salmon Arm and the Peace Pole? What ultimately happened to the World Peace University Society?

It relocated.

Where?

Costa Rica! The very place Bill Clinton touts as a model for sustainability. The group formed in Salmon Arm now sports a new name, as yet another NGO (non-government organization). Talk about momentum! This whole evolution took place in a mere twenty-three years! One major accelerant sprayed onto this fire is the discovery that there is a great deal of money to be made by creating financial means of uniting global economies; for example buying and selling of "carbon credits."

Don't forget the remarks of the teenaged girl who said, "All religions that are not harmonious with The New Age must be eliminated." Has there been any progress on that front?

Just last week, Rick Warren, who gave the invocation at President Obama's first inauguration, criticized him:

> The pastor of California-based Saddleback Church made these remarks to the Huffington Post, saying that Obama is "absolutely" unfriendly to religion and his administration's policies have "intentionally infringed upon religious liberties."[11]

In an interview with Marc Lamont Hill of Huff Post Live on Wednesday, Warren took issue with the contraception mandate issued by the Department of Health and Human Services earlier this year:

"'I believe…you should have a right to be able to practice your belief without the government forcing you to do something different," said Warren. "If they made a law where you have to sell contraception if you're Catholic, well then how about a law to Jewish Rabbis that says you have to sell pork in every deli?" Warren also talked about a bill in San Francisco that would ban circumcision, to which the pastor warned that it could eventually lead to the banning of baptism.[12]

I showed how Narrative construction is crucial for change agents to accomplish their goals. I talked at length of what I believe to be the danger of replacing systematic theology with Narrative Theology. Does re-telling "the story" while downplaying certainty really matter?

I remember an experiment that took place in an Abnormal Psychology class I took in the early 1970s. It was a large class which met in an amphitheater.

The professor chose six volunteers. Five of them were sent out of the classroom to a secure area. Addressing the first volunteer, the professor then explained. "I am now going to show you a slide which you will look at and memorize. After two minutes I will turn it off and then invite the next person back into the classroom, and you are to simply tell him what you saw."

Here is what the slide showed:

- It was a passenger car on a train.
- The conductor (in uniform) was entering the car.
- He was looking at the watch in his hand.
- A drunk had passed out on the floor of the car.
- Seated near the drunk was a white woman with a baby in her arms.
- Finally there was a young black man steadying himself by holding on to the car's overhead strap.

The one student who actually saw the slide told the second one what he saw, with minor disparities. Then number two told number three. Then number three told number four. One at a time they passed on the information until number five told number six this report of what was on the slide he had never actually seen. Here is what he reported:

- It was a subway car.
- A black man had just stabbed another man who was bleeding to death on the floor.
- He had his hand raised to stab a white woman who was protecting her baby.
- Just then a uniformed policeman came in and was just about shoot!

Mind you, this was only retelling a story five times in the span of one class period! Note also that this was in the 1960s at the height of the racial tensions following the assassination of Martin Luther King Jr. With no coaching whatever from the professor, the cultural issues of the day so affected the participants that the facts of the story—the objective truth disappeared in the span of about a half an hour.

Without a written certified account of what actually happened, the story evolved rapidly, and it was clearly subject to the biases of those who retold it. If this could happen in a fifty-minute class, I think it becomes evident that the retelling of a narrative, no matter how well-crafted it is, is bound to result in a gross misrepresentation of the original events.

Emergent leader Brian McClaren has been "retelling the story" for a number of years and his retelling has become increasingly vague when it comes to gay marriage. We now learn that he has presided over a "commitment" ceremony for his gay son.

I showed how I believe the devil has a plan to use all this "repackaging of the gospel story." His narrative is served by the current religious chaos. One day, perhaps sooner than we think, his narrative will be embodied in human form. This miracle worker will probably appear as some sort of transformational change agent—an architect of narratives, if you will.

Robert Ingersoll was one of the most famous opponents of biblical Christianity who ever lived. I picture him as the Bill Maher of his day, only with much more civility and a better command of the language.

L.W. Munhall, who wrote *Anti-Higher Criticism-Testimony to the Infallibility of the Bible* in 1893, was very familiar with Ingersoll and his anti-biblical arguments. He cited one exchange in which Ingersoll was asked, "How come you don't still write against the Bible?" Ingersoll replied, "Why the seminary professors and the pastors are doing a much better job than I in discrediting the Scriptures."[13]

I read a number of books by Rev. Munhall. His work in defending the inerrancy of Scripture was highly significant in his day. Munhall held annual conferences in which pastors and scholars met to write articles and deliver messages in defense of an inerrant Bible.

In one of his essays, delivered at the annual conference, he wrote this powerful illustration:

Yonder, upon the bosom of the granite hills, is a fountain. By some unknown and untraceable conduit it is connected with some greater fountain amid the glaciers and eternal snows of loftier heights. From its subterranean depths an inexhaustible source…it pours forth its floods of pure, clear, life-giving water.

Stretching away from the base of these solemn hills, far beyond the horizon is an arid, desert waste. Evidences of life are few in all its vast expanse, and it lies desolate under storm and calm. But enterprising men gather the floods of this fountain into a great reservoir, and thence carry it by pipes and ditches, abroad over the dusty plain; and soon teeming fields, throbbing with life, everywhere greet the eye.…

The word of God is a fountain, connected how, you and I know not, with the fountain of perennial youth in the heart of The Eternal. *The church of God is but a reservoir for receiving these life-giving floods; and forth from this reservoir these waters are to continually flow to make glad the waste places…our business is to keep the conduits clean and unobstructed, and let the waters flow on forever.*[14] (Emphasis mine.)

I have attempted to be faithful in sharing what I believe the Lord has shown me about the times in which we live, and the extent of the debate of whether or not we can trust the inerrancy of the Bible. My intent is "to keep the conduits clean and unobstructed." I acknowledge that there are good men and women who operate in integrity who will disagree with much of what I have written. Still others will critique how I wrote it. I know that there is great nuance involved in biblical Criticism.

This issue of biblical inerrancy is an issue that transcends our times, and has enormous impact on those generations who will follow.

The Cross at Ground Zero means a lot to those who worked on "the Pile." I was there the day they found it. The atmosphere was electric. "Did you hear what they found? It's a miracle!" Hardened firefighters and crane operators had tears well up as they described the cross.

Guideposts magazine carried this inspiring account by the worker who discovered the cross:

I'm an excavation laborer and a member of union local 731. Pick-and-shovel work is my trade. I live in New Jersey, but I'm a New York City native, Brooklyn-born and bred.

After the Towers collapsed, my city was hurting. When I heard they needed guys like me for search-and-rescue work at Ground Zero, I couldn't get there fast enough.

I'd seen the news coverage, but that didn't prepare me for the reality. Down there it was like hell on earth. Fires burned out of control. Destroyed vehicles littered the streets. Everything was blanketed with dust; the air was filled with a choking stench. I soaked a bandanna with water before wrapping it around my head to cover my nose and mouth. I went to work wondering if I'd be able to get through this.

Six firefighters and I entered World Trade Center building six, which had been flattened by Tower One. We took a smoke-filled stairway down into the garage levels, searching for survivors. There were no cries for help, no signs of life. We spray-painted orange Xs to indicate where we'd searched and to help us find our way back.

After 12 hours of searching, we'd recovered three bodies. By then I was exhausted, but I couldn't quit. "Think I'll take a look over there," I told the firemen, motioning toward the remains of the lobby atrium.

Picking my way through the massive piles of debris, I peered into what had become a sort of grotto. Illuminated by the pale light of dawn were shapes ... crosses. What? How did these get here? The largest was about 20 feet high. It must have weighed a couple of tons.

In that little grotto I felt a strange sense of peace and stillness. I could almost hear God saying, *The terrible thing done at this site was meant for evil. But I will turn it to good. Have faith. I am here.* I fell to my knees in front of the largest cross. Tears came, and I couldn't stop them. I cried like a baby.[15]

Not everyone, however, was happy about the cross and the prominence it would have in the memorial. On December 6, 2012, *World Net Daily* reported:

Atheists claim Ground Zero cross sickens them. Lawsuit says victims suffer dyspepsia, headache, anxiety, anguish...[16]

ACLJ chief Jay Sekulow sums up the complaint:

"The plaintiffs, and each of them, are suffering, and will continue to suffer damages, both physical and emotional, from the existence of the challenged cross," the lawsuit American Atheists v. Port Authority of New York and New Jersey states. "Named plaintiffs have suffered…dyspepsia, symptoms of depression, headaches, anxiety, and mental pain and anguish from the knowledge that they are made to feel officially excluded from the ranks of citizens who were directly injured by the 9/11 attack."[16]

The cross always separates. It will always be a source of scandal and controversy. Downplaying its significance by devaluing the Bible will not change that fact. As Erwin Lutzer so powerfully pointed out, the German people stood between two crosses. We in America are facing a similar dilemma.

Reverend Munhall perhaps says best what I believe. He quotes Bishop Ryle who commented on the controversy surrounding the doctrine of inerrancy:

I'll take the plenary verbal theory with all its difficulties rather than the doubt. I accept the difficulties and humbly wait for their solution, but while I wait I am standing on a rock.[17]

FOURTEEN

ANYBODY SEEN A TRUMPET?

"The church will remain ineffective if it continues to have as its spokesmen the people who have been falling all over each other to be 'relevant.' Ages of faith are not marked by dialogue but by proclamation."

DR. JOHN WARWICK MONTGOMERY

"The Christian is not embarrassed in the least that he cannot explain everything about God. God would not be God if this were possible. One never worships what he can understand. It is only when he gets beyond the realm of his own comprehension that he bows his head and lifts his hands in worship."

DR. GUY P. DUFFIELD AND DR. NATHANIEL VAN CLEAVE

"It has taken me all of my life to learn what not to play."

DIZZY GILLESPIE

Anyone seen a trumpet?" These words appeared in the first chapter of God's Inerrant Word: An International Symposium on the Trustworthiness of Scripture. Dr. John Warwick Montgomery in the opening essay of this valuable defense of the doctrine of inerrancy starts with a familiar passage of Scripture.

If the trumpet gives an uncertain sound...who shall prepare himself to the battle?

1 COR. 14:8, KJV

The observation he made then in 1974 is particularly applicable to our day. I was struck by how similar the debate in the late 1970s was to the one we are engaged in today along with the relentless devaluing of the Scriptures that is taking place. Montgomery wrote:

> In large regions of the ecclesiastical landscape the warriors appear totally incapable of identifying the battle lines. The silence is ominous: hardly anyone seems to be able to find the trumpet much less to play certain sounds on it.[1]

Another chaplain and I once started a forest fire. That's right. He and I were training with a battalion of Marines in the Arizona desert. It was 120 degrees. "Don't worry," the Gunny said, "It's a dry heat!" We were with them as they qualified with the fifty-caliber machine gun. "Want to try this, chaplain?"

While in a prone firing position, I put in my ear protection and squeezed off some rounds from a truly fearsome weapon nicknamed "the saw." It was sobering to feel and see what such a weapon can do. My chaplain colleague hit the target (a derelict tank in the distance) and the tracer round ignited the tinder-dry grass. The winds kicked up and we had a situation on our hands.

As the incident unfolded, and after my boss went to try and help fight the fire, someone handed me the radio. I have no idea why. I was totally out of my area of expertise. I had never spoken on a radio in my life. As the troops tried to fight the fire, I was to call higher authority and let them know what was unfolding.

It must have looked like a lost episode of Gomer Pyle. I think I said, "Hello this is Chaplain Jenkins speaking." My fellow chaplain and the other Marines never let me forget how dumb I sounded.

There is, you see, a need for crystal clarity in combat communications or in other emergencies. There must be a certain, unambiguous message delivered in precise and understandable terms. For instance when calling in the coordinates for an artillery strike—if you are confused about what has been said—you never say *repeat...* unless you mean for more rounds to be fired at the same coordinates. You say, "Say again."

I thought of this incident when I re-read Dr. Montgomery's seminal article. I needed to be clear in a crisis. Because I never learned how to use a field radio, I ran the risk of causing some serious confusion, and even some injuries. The troops needed clear authoritative guidance, and due to my lack of precision they stood to have mixed signals with potentially dire consequences.

Leaders are held to a higher standard. This is a well-known and documented New Testament principle. Dr. Montgomery rightly calls leaders to account. He put his finger squarely on the mark with this indictment of those who should know better, the preachers and teachers.

> The church will remain ineffective if it continues to have as its spokesmen the people who have been falling all over each other to be "relevant." Ages of faith are not marked by dialogue but by proclamation.[2]

I can't say it any better. We have today legions of bloggers and pastors who seem to make it their business to, as Dr. Montgomery characterized their predecessors from the seventies, "fall all over each other to be relevant." There is a possible explanation for this. It may be as simple as the need to be affirmed and recognized. I sense in many of the Emergent writers an almost desperate attempt to prove that they are relevant and "hip" (whatever that means).

I say yet again that Emergent Church leaders leave the distinct impression that the mere proclamation of God's Word is not enough to reach postmoderns. Think of what this says about God. It hints that somehow His Word is deficient and that He meant for us to act as editors and redactors of His Word.

The shift away from declaring propositional truth and the relentless backing away from an unashamed declaration of the claims of Christ as the only way of salvation is evidence of a lack of confidence in the power of God's Word.

I had the privilege of studying under Dr. Montgomery in the late 1970s and I was struck by the sheer logic of his presentations. He makes the muddy water clear with this statement to do with the argument about inerrancy,

Evidence for biblical inerrancy whether viewed from the angle of Textual Criticism or from the more general perspective of apologetics is never itself inerrant, but this by no means makes the inerrancy claim irrational. Warfield (like Fuller) is perfectly willing to admit that his case is a probability case, yet (unlike Fuller) he affirms the inerrancy of the bible in *all* matters to which it refers— not just to those "germane to salvation" (whatever they may be).

Why? Because he correctly observes the evidence that Christ (God Himself incarnate) held to exactly this inerrancy view of Scripture "is about as great in amount and weight as 'probably' evidence can be made and this warrants conviction on our part."[3] [Emphasis mine.]

Montgomery's warning in the seventies has proven to be prophetic. With the advent of social media and instant Internet communication, we now have a scenario in which people can express themselves in a much more sarcastic fashion due to the relative anonymity afforded by blogs.

It appears that in the anonymous environment of cyber space, people are emboldened to say things they would never dare to utter in person. Afforded the luxury of such a lack of accountability, they can push the envelope and delve into areas that were deemed heretical just one generation ago.

I notice, however, that in times of threat, there is not so much traffic in the more extreme kinds of speculations that characterize some of the Emergent Church "conversation" today. Dr. Montgomery concluded his essay, *"Biblical Inerrancy: What Is at Stake?"* with these sobering remarks. (Keep in mind they were written in 1974!):

Perhaps we are slow to realize what is at stake in the conflict over the extent of biblical authority because we do not feel, as some have felt in our time, the breath of the antichrist, and the pressure of demonic forces that would twist the world into his unholy image.

A theologian well acquainted with the German scene—and certainly no fundamentalist—makes the following highly significant observation.

In the years of Nazi persecution, the confessional church ministers biblical interpretation was a near fundamentalism—"Es steht geschrieben… It is written" was his answer to every question. A few years later, Bultmann's radical criticism was a burning issue in Germany. But only after General Eisenhower's armies had liberated Western Germany. Probably any church in a situation of crisis reverts to as near fundamentalism as makes no odds.[4]

I have often reflected on the fact that in a time of dire national threat, pastors and churches are not as likely to question the inerrancy of the Bible. In fact, they tend to want it to be totally reliable. Dr. Montgomery's conclusion is extremely apropos to our day.

Right now I am thinking back to the climate in the US in the days immediately following September 11, 2001. There was a sort of national suspension of cynicism. We were, it seemed, all on the same page. We took pride in our distinct identity as a nation. We made no apology about our position in the world. Sadly, within a year things returned to their former state.

Dr. Montgomery condenses the issue down to its essence. He answers the question posed by the essay, "What is at stake?"

Does this not say something terribly important as to what is at stake in the inerrancy issue? In crisis, there is no alternative to proclamation which "makes no odds." Under such conditions, anything less than total assurance in Christian proclamation is betrayal of Christ and sure defeat. BUT HOW CAN ONE SAY "IT IS WRITTEN" WITHOUT A SCRIPTURE THAT IS ENTIRELY TRUSTWORTHY? [Emphasis mine.] We need to become aware that all of life is really a crisis in a sinful world where the battle between Christ and the forces of evil never ceases for a moment.

What is at stake? Your effectiveness in that battle... and mine...
Let us not tarnish and corrode our only weapon—the sword of the
Spirit which is the Word of God.[5]

One of the most dog-eared books in my library is one entitled *Foundations of Pentecostal Theology.* I can't tell you how many times I pulled out this valuable reference tool to refresh my grasp on the doctrine of inerrancy. Drs. Duffield and Van Cleave have done the Body of Christ a great service. In plain simple terms, they spell out what the Bible says about itself, what Jesus says about its reliability, and what others have said in its defense.

I love the clarity of this remark. Quoting a writer named Chafer, they write,

> The Christian is not embarrassed in the least that he cannot explain everything about God. God would not be God if this were possible. One never worships what he can understand. It is only when he gets beyond the realm of his own comprehension that he bows his head and lifts his hands in worship.[6]

I agree wholeheartedly. If the Word of God is in fact "alive and active," as the writer of Hebrews reports, then we are left with a choice. If, as Jesus declared, "heaven and earth will pass away but my word will never pass away" is actually true, then we would do well to treat the Bible as being different than any other literature. If Jesus meant it when he said "My words are spirit and they are life" then we would do well to not give to ourselves the freedom of "explaining what God meant," based on our puny knowledge base. In fact we would do well to fear God and his warnings about tampering with His Words.

Duffield and Van Cleave conclude,

> The mistake is to try and explain the inexplicable and to fathom the unfathomable. The means or process of inspiration is a mystery of the providence of God, but the results of this process is a verbal

(the words) plenary (the extent) to all parts equally inerrant (error-less) and authoritative record.[7]

Compare this humble confidence to a recent op-ed piece that appeared in the *Youngstown Vindicator*. The author is Jeff Kunerth of McClatchy Press:

In his first class of the fall semester, University of Central Florida professor Charles Negy suggested to his cross-cultural psychology students that they might want to read his email to last semester's class that went viral on the Internet—twice.

In the email that created a sensation at the time and again just weeks before the fall term began, Negy chastised the devout Christian student who told the rest of the class to ignore the professor questioning their religious beliefs.

"Students in my class who openly proclaimed that Christianity is the most valid religion, as some of you did last class, portrayed precisely what religious bigotry is. Bigots—racial bigots or religious bigots—never question their prejudices and bigotry. They are convinced their beliefs are correct."[8]

Catch the significance of that. A professor belittles a Christian for asserting that his religion is universally true. He calls him a bigot. Now I realize that this occurred in a secular university and that proselytizing in a cross cultural psychology class was probably not looked upon kindly by the professor. I wonder, though, if this professor would be quite so strident in his opposition if this was a Muslim student advocating for the implementation of Sharia law. I very much doubt he would have had the nerve to call a Muslim student a bigot for stating that Islam is binding on everyone. The good professor brings his bias, as Jeff Kunerth points out:

Many blame professors such as Negy for contributing to a generation that has largely turned its back on organized religion. The

"Millennials" ages 18 to 29 are far less religious than their parents. About 25 percent of them have no religious affiliation compared with 13 percent of baby boomers at the same age.

"I think the negative criticism (of Christians) is much more in academia than the general population," said Clark Whitten, senior pastor of Grace Church Orlando in Longwood, Fla. "There is a patronizing way that is offensive when they make you feel small-minded to believe in faith." Whitten said the student was right to stand up in defense of Christianity: "I don't see it as bigotry. I see it as the truth."

Negy said he never tries to convince his students they should change their beliefs or adopt his views on religion, but to learn to think for themselves—as he did when he was their age.

Negy grew up as Southern Baptist in Texas and didn't begin to question his religious beliefs until he was a college student in Spain and learned about Islam. He found himself thinking, "Is Jesus the true prophet or is Mohammed? What proof is there that either is?"

And then I realized, "Oh, my God, I've been believing this for 25 years because everyone around me believes it," Negy said. "I understand if you are raised to never think critically, and question those beliefs, you are shocked that anyone would question that validity. That's what I want to do in my class."[9]

Questioning the validity of simple Christian faith is not limited to the college or university. Some self-described "progressive" pastors are questioning what they perceive to be the uncritical, simplistic doctrines taught to them by their predecessors.

In this book I have done my best to map out what I feel has taken place over the last few decades. I have observed denomination after denomination begin to flirt with the notion that accommodation to a "postmodern culture" is the only means of survival for the church.

Like Francis Schaeffer warned, and Harold Lindsell predicted, John MacArthur and others including myself now chronicle as having taken place, the wheels are coming off and this whole mess is now spinning out of control. The Great Down Grade that Charles Spurgeon predicted is resulting in whole denominations hurtling down the winding hairpin curves at breakneck speed. Dr. Criswell and others tried to warn their respective church bodies that this would happen.

No Christian who has lived in Los Angeles in the last forty years would be unfamiliar with the familiar strings of praise music that introduced the radio program "The Word for Today," a broadcast of Calvary Chapel. Pastor Chuck Smith preached the Word to millions every day. Calvary Chapel has been a mighty tool in the hands of God in these last decades. Pastor Rob Verdyen of Calvary Corvallis (Oregon) succinctly sums up their approach to preaching, *"Simply teaching the Word...simply."*

In a book released in 2011, Paul Smith, Pastor Chuck's brother preaches an urgent message to any pastor who is trying to understand what has been happening in recent years. His title says it all, *New Evangelicalism: The New World Order.*

I was immediately interested in reading this book for two reasons:

- His experience is so similar to my own.
- His line of reasoning and chronicling of the events at Fuller Seminary describe my experience there. (I earned my doctorate at Fuller.)

I concur with his conclusion, one which is on the minds of many, but few have had the courage to utter out loud:

Our current generation has witnessed two eschatological markers with our own eyes. The first one was the Jews returning to the Promised Land and forming the first nation of Israel in 1948. The second marker is the Emergent Church paradigm that gave birth and will inadvertently host, through accommodation and compromise and a postmodern mindset a platform suitable for the coming one world religion as clearly prophesied in the Bible.[10]

He challenges us with this exhortation:

Our generation needs to rediscover and embrace these twin sufficiencies: First, God's inerrant Word, and second the power and ministry of The Holy Spirit to open our minds.[11]

I was at Fuller Seminary when the Church Growth Movement was in full bloom. Sometimes it seemed that all we heard were statistics and strategies. The new tools deemed essential for pastors were a strong entrepreneurial spirit and good business sense. Especially needed was the knack of cultivating a church culture which pandered to "what the customer wanted." (One instructor used those very words.)

It was at Fuller that I first came across the writings of George Barna (author of *Marketing the Church*). It was there that I first heard the name Peter Drucker (the management guru who Rick Warren credits as his mentor).

One of the warning signs to me that our denomination was taking a dangerous wrong turn down a steep grade was the plethora of Church Growth books being recommended to pastors and the kinds of speakers that were engaged to speak to our conventions. I noticed that over time the roster included speakers whose backgrounds included advertising, polling, sociology, psychology, and management.

It was as if there were some grand concession that the church "as is" was inadequate. More and more of our leaders now have advanced degrees in disciplines other than theology…i.e., strategic leadership, management, and yes, even marketing and human resource management.

I remember sitting at a conference years ago at the Beaverton Foursquare Church. Pastor Jim Cymbala, pastor of Brooklyn Tabernacle Church was the speaker. He stopped his remarks, stared out at the pastors and their wives and said words that hit me like a hammer.

"I am speaking by the Spirit of prophecy now. TECHNICIANS HAVE INVADED THE CHURCH!"

I knew then that what I had been observing and reacting to over the years was indeed spiritual. Even as I sat in those classes at Fuller, I had the sense that not everything I was learning was necessarily the Spirit of God at work, but perhaps another spirit. This emphasis on numbers and surveys, and personality profiles and gifts inventories, and demonstrable results, and polls, put the attention not on the Risen Lord and what He has done, but on technology and what man can do.

Years ago something happened at the church I pastored in Oregon. Our sanctuary was an old elementary school. The Quonset hut that served as the school gym became our sanctuary and the large classrooms served our Sunday school nicely. We were located out in the country, and it was not unusual to see deer and coyotes on the back of the property. Some other forms of wildlife were also at home in and around our building. Snakes! I hate snakes!

After I was there for a few years, I noticed that the entry to the basement (where the school cafeteria was located) had a big crack in the foundation. I had to clean away the leaves from the grate there or the basement would flood. One year I noticed a little snake pop his head out of the crack. I made note of it as I backed away…did I mention I hate snakes? I didn't do anything. It was just a *little* snake.

The next time I noticed something was later that year. A much larger snake slithered out of the same crack, and then another and then another. I panicked and grabbed a shovel and started to kill the snakes. After that very unpleasant battle, I got some rock and filled the hole. You see, the snakes were living very close to where the kids were located.

The belief in an inerrant Bible has been, until fairly recently in our history, a given. A lesson I learned in the Word of God shortly after the *snake in the crack affair* (as it came to be known) made a lasting impression on me. It had to do with the period when the Jews were allowed to go back to rebuild the Temple and to rebuild the walls of Jerusalem.

THE SNAKE IN THE CRACKED FOUNDATION

The people of God had been overrun and banished into captivity. This happened because they had abandoned the worship of the one true God, Yahweh, and began to intermingle with other religions—pagan religions with detestable practices. Some of the pagan religions' worship involved sacrificing children in the fire. Other religious rites involved prostitution as part of their "worship."

Forget that for a moment. The real sin was that God expressly forbade them to intermingle like that. He said "Thus says the Lord." They said, "We prefer..." He even warned them time and again that there would be dire consequences to such disobedience. As a result they were banished to Babylon and Jerusalem was laid waste. A merciful God after a period of seventy years made a way for the people to return. "In the first year of Cyrus king of Persia, in order to fulfill the word of the Lord spoken by Jeremiah, the Lord moved the heart of Cyrus king of Persia to make a proclamation..." (Ezra 1:1).

He basically gave the Jews carte blanche to go back and rebuild Jerusalem. It was a second chance, even after they had embraced pagan defilement. The Bible records the response:

> Then the family heads of Judah and Benjamin, and the priests and
> Levites—everyone whose heart God had moved—prepared to go
> up and build the house of the Lord in Jerusalem (Ezra 1:5).

Ezra, a contemporary of Nehemiah, was used by God to head up the task of rebuilding the Temple, whereas Nehemiah was tasked with rebuilding the wall of Jerusalem. The return from Babylon has been referred to by some as "the second Exodus." One major difference, however, is highly significant. This one from Babylon is less impressive than the return from Egypt because *only a remnant chose to leave Babylon.*

I take that to mean that the others were at least comfortable enough by means of assimilation and accommodation and intermarriage that they "preferred" Babylon. One of the main adversaries both Nehemiah and Ezra had to deal with was Sanballat, the Horonite. He opposed them at every turn. He used lies, threats, intrigues—anything to try and stop this work of rebuilding.

Chapter 4 of Ezra reveals that the "enemies of Judah" who opposed the rebuilding were Samaritans. They said, "We, like you, seek your God and have been sacrificing to him." That was only partially true. It was also true that the religion of the Samaritans involved the worship of all sorts of gods, and they were probably taking up the worship of the Jewish god as only one god among many, a local religious cultural/accommodation if you will.

Tobiah, the Ammonite, and Sanballat, the Horonite, led the opposition to Ezra and Nehemiah. The name "Tobiah" may be an honorific title for a high ranking Persian official. The Bible dictionary suggests that he was half Jewish as his name suggests "God is good." His close association with Sanballat, the governor of Samaria, suggests that he was Sanballat's deputy.

If the Holy Spirit does in fact quicken the Bible as we read it, and if He does speak to us from His Word, allow me to offer what I feel I was shown about these two individuals. The Jews were to have nothing to do with the Ammonites. In fact the Ammonites were specifically designated by God to Moses and to Joshua as perennial adversaries because they refused to help the Jews during the Exodus. An Ammonite had not only been tolerated. He had rooms and influence in the Temple!

Sanballat was a Horonite, and one root of that word Horonite comes from an unused root pronounced *Khoor* probably meaning to bore; the crevice of a serpent; the cell of a prison-hole.[12] Think back to the snake in the crack incident.

Once the book of the law was found and was read aloud, both the leaders and newly returned community faced a dilemma:

On that day the Book of Moses was read aloud in the hearing of the people and there it was found that no Ammonite or Moabite should ever be admitted to the assembly of God because they had not met the Israelites with food and water, but had hired Balaam to call down a curse on them.

The ensuing passage is a sad commentary:

But Eliashib the High Priest had been put in charge of the store rooms of the house of our God. He was closely associated with Tobiah, and had provided him with a large room formerly used to store grain offerings and incense and temple articles and also the tithes of grain, new wine and oil prescribed for the Levites, singers and gatekeepers as well as the contributions for the priests (Neh.13).

I said that there was something in the historical account of what Ezra and Nehemiah did that was germane to this whole discussion about the Word of God. When the Scriptures were rediscovered and taken seriously, once Nehemiah learned that Tobiah had an apartment in the Temple, he threw Tobiah's things out. Later in the book we read he would get so mad that he punched some people and tore out their hair. What was it that made him so mad?

He discovered that all the accommodation to the pagan culture resulted in the fact that an entire generation of the Hebrew children did not even know their own language anymore (Neh. 13:23–28).

Our passage of Scripture goes on to say that Nehemiah found out that one of the sons of Joiada (the High Priest) was Sanballat's son-in-law! The NIV Study Bible has this note on this particular passage:

> The high Priest was not to marry a foreigner. The expulsion of Joiada's son followed either this special ban or the general prohibition against intermarriage. The union described in this verse was especially rankling to Nehemiah in light of Sanballat's enmity.… Josephus, in his *Antiquities of the Jews* 11:72, recorded that an almost identical episode involving a marriage between the daughter of Sanballat of Samaria and the brother of the Jewish High Priest took place over a century later in the time of Alexander the Great.

Such carelessness, such conformity to the surrounding pagan influence, had all but negated the possibility of a clear prophetic voice being uttered or understood.

WHO CONFORMS TO WHAT?

When I was a boy I had rheumatic fever. I lost a whole year of school and had to have a tutor come to our house. God bless my mom. She did every-thing to keep me current, and to keep me motivated. I talked her into allow-ing me to take trumpet lessons.

There were no such things as home owner associations in those days, but if they had existed, one would have formed on Bryson Street, and they would have sent a delegation to ask my family to move. I was awful! The screeching sounded like a chain-smoking goose with asthma. I learned one tune vaguely—extremely vaguely. It was something akin to "When the saints go marching in." I played it over and over again. I just couldn't get my lips right.

My friend, Lauren Johnson, an accomplished musician and trumpet teacher, explained to me what the problem might have been. I didn't have a proper embouchure. The embouchure is the process of forming ones mouth on the mouthpiece in order to produce a distinct sound. It takes muscles and practice, lots of practice to form your mouth onto the fixed instrument. This to me is what is wrong with the current fascination with contextualizing and de-constructing the Bible. It is as if a trumpet student was saying, "I will conform the instrument to me" rather than the other way around. The form required to produce a clear note has already been determined. It falls to me whether or not I will submit to the preordained instrument's requirements.

For years, my wife, Judy, was the accompanist for the local high school music program. She was classically trained by The Royal Conservatory of Music in Canada. She is amazing. She can pick up a complicated piece of music, sit down, and nail it the first time.

She tells the story of how in the first days of a new school year those wishing to play horns are given only the mouthpiece until they can properly demonstrate the correct embouchure. She told me it was really comical to see all these kids running around making sounds like wounded ducks.

I have never heard of a drowning man debating the principle of buoy-ancy before he grabbed the ring tossed to him. I say unhesitatingly that the proclamation of the gospel requires our belief and our trust, and yes, our obedience, not our expertise. Like the music students learning the embouchure before they proceed in their music studies, we would do well to not focus on nuance so much as the childlike faith needed to conform our "mouthpieces" to the word of God instead of working hard to conform God's Word to an increasingly corrupt culture.

It's not whether it is "Blue Like Jazz" or Edgy or New Age or Big Band or Southern Gospel for that matter. If it doesn't conform to the One whose music has already been written out, it's just noise.

Newsbusters.org ran a *Newsweek* magazine cover on their blog. It appeared in the online magazine dated Jan. 18, 2013. The writer, Brent Baker, reported:

Conservatives have long joked that the national press corps see Barack Obama as the second coming of Jesus Christ. Today, *Newsweek*—at least what's left of it, an online product for tablets and e-readers—made it official. Next to a side shot of Obama's head, the "Inauguration 2013" cover story pronounced: "The Second Coming."

It's an article by long-time *Newsweek* veteran Evan Thomas, who left the magazine after Tina Brown took over from the Washington Post Company and folded the debt-ridden publication into her Daily Beast site.

The January 18, 2013, online magazine, was posted Friday to those who were subscribers to the printed magazine.

Linking God and Obama isn't new for Thomas, once an Assistant Managing Editor and Washington Bureau Chief for the former weekly. Back in June of 2009, naturally on MSNBC, Thomas asserted, "In a way, Obama's standing above the country, above—above the world. He's sort of God. He's going to bring all different sides together."[13]

Do I believe this is some sort of proof that the president in the Antichrist? No. Do I think it shows a measure of contempt for the church? Yes.

On the day I submitted this manuscript to the printer, I heard a fascinating remark from a news anchor conducting an interview on the day after President Obama's second Inauguration. He was pressing his guest to comment on the obvious liberal/progressive tone in the president's speech. Finally, he said with some measure of alarm, "DOESN'T THIS REPRESENT A WATERSHED event in the history of American politics?"[14] [Emphasis mine...I am hearkening back to Francis Schaeffer's remarks about the watershed.] In an eerily fitting coincidence, I noted this interview took place on the fortieth anniversary of Roe v. Wade, and again I hearkened back to Schaeffer's remarks.

I have sat at the bedside of many people who were about to die. As I read the Word of God to them, I have thought more than once how obscene it would be for me to boldly read these things at a time like someone's death if there was any doubt as to the reliability or certainty of the words contained in the Bible.

As I accompanied family members to actually see the horror that was Ground Zero, I often quoted Scripture. When we walked up to the staging area that had been prepared for the families to see "The Pile," many of them fainted. Some vomited. One lady pulled out clumps of her hair till her scalp bled.

How cruel it would have been for me to bring anything but a certain unambiguous Word from God to a moment like that. Those folks experienced the supernatural comfort promised in the Word because it was in fact the very Words of God that I spoke.

Not one person complained that I spoke God's Word. It is only in times of relative ease, when we are challenged about some behavior to which we prefer to cling that we become irritated with certain passages that we deem to be "culturally irrelevant" or hateful.

I wrote this book in an effort to raise these simple questions:

- Does it matter that we are beginning to ignore whole parts of God's revealed will?
- Do we have permission, as some seem to have concluded, to

pick and choose which passages are inspired and which are mere cultural mores?

- Will God judge us according to His Word?

Pastors, are you acquiescing just to get along? Are you teaching the people entrusted to your care that God's Word is only partly inspired? Are you about to join the scores of ministers who have chosen not to talk about controversial subjects anymore?

Chaplains, will you say "yes sir" and perform gay marriage ceremonies, even though you know what the Bible says about this subject?

Christians, will you just go along as the abortion industry continues to slaughter innocents? Where is the line over which you will not cross? Does it even exist anymore?

Who will rescue those perishing at Cape Disappointment? Is shipwrecked faith the new normal? I pray that somehow I have edified those who may have felt that they were alone in noticing this dangerous trend. I also pray that I have made others uncomfortable by pressing the issue. At a congressional hearing investigating the murder of American Diplomat Chris Stevens and the brave security personnel in Benghazi, Libya, who tried to save his life, Secretary of State Hilary Clinton angrily attacked Senator Ron Johnson:

> Clinton responded to Sen. Ron Johnson's questioning over the reason for the attack, saying, "Was it because of a protest or was it because of guys out for a walk one night who decided they'd go kill some Americans? WHAT DIFFERENCE, AT THIS POINT, DOES IT MAKE? It is our job to figure out what happened and do everything we can to prevent it from ever happening again."[15] [Emphasis mine.]

She deftly avoided even coming close to actually answering the question about the phony video protest story fabricated by the White House. Her answer, and more to the point her tone, underscored what I have been trying to communicate in this book. Talking points, and narratives and optics have trumped the truth yet again. She was in essence smugly saying "What does it matter if we lied? Let's get on with the narrative we have prepared for this "conversation." I wonder how the family members of those dead Americans felt when they heard her say that?

In answering the question "Anybody seen a trumpet?" I can answer "yes." I dare to think that perhaps I have gotten the embouchure right at last, and that a trumpet blast has gone forth that will effect positive change in the Body of Christ.

Alexander Solzhenitsyn, himself imprisoned in the Gulags for speaking truth to power, wrote this powerful observation:

The simple step of a courageous individual is not to take part in the lie. One word of truth outweighs the world.[16]

I close with the words of Martin Luther,

Peace if possible, the truth at any rate.[17]

EPILOGUE

"But while men slept his enemy came and sowed."

MATTHEW 13:25

don't know how you picture the devil. Some see him as a sinister creature with pointed horns, wearing a red spandex suit with a pitchfork in his hand. Still others imagine him to be a ghoulish, half snake/dragon sort of creature. I have come to picture him sitting at a corner office in Manhattan as the head of an advertising agency.

He is the father of lies...the progenitor...the crafter. Don't we call someone who carefully crafts something a fabricator? There is a great deal of forethought and design that goes into a good fabrication. Advertisers are willing to invest great amounts of time and energy and expense to create a mindset.

Adolf Hitler was surrounded mostly by totally loyal functionaries who would do whatever he commanded without question. They were not as a rule educated men. He had only two in his inner circle who had advanced degrees. One was the architect, Albert Speer; the other was a little man with a limp who had a PhD in philosophy and another in literature. His name was Joseph Goebbels.

Dr. Goebbels succeeded in changing the mindset of a nation in a relatively short period of time. So called "normal" everyday Germans went from doing business with and socializing with their Jewish neighbors to shouting epithets at them...comparing them to rats as they were taken away in cattle cars to be incinerated. The most amazing thing of all is that "the little doctor" accomplished this feat in less than a decade!

How? How did Goebbels create an alternative universe, and get most people to buy into it? I would offer that he paid attention in school when the first grade teacher taught the lesson on seeds.

You remember it, don't you? Miss Crabtree had all her little charges put on their aprons and get their little Dixie cups filled with dirt and some white granules. She then passed out bean seeds or pumpkin seeds and had the kids "plant the seed." Then they watered it and placed the cups up on the window ledge so they could get some sunlight. The class watched every day until the green sprout popped out and began to grow.

The seeds of rabid anti-Semitism were already available. After the end of WWI and the Treaty of Versailles which the Germans resented bitterly, people were suffering economically, inflation was rampant, and they needed something or someone to blame.

Goebbels, who understood philosophy and literature, used his expertise to begin *methodically* identifying the Jews as the cause for all the post war suffering. A note here about the word "methodical." In Paul's letter to the Ephesians, he reminds the church that they have to take up all the armor of God in order to resist or stand against the *schemes* of the devil. The Greek word Paul used for schemes is *methodias*. One Greek dictionary uses the words "travesty" and "trickery" and "lie in wait" to convey its meaning.

Goebbels began by means of press releases and articles and movies and broadcasts to portray the Jews as the embodiment of evil in the world and the direct cause for the plight of the German people. He had a complicit press. In fact, the media of the day was totally controlled by the Nazis and nothing was allowed to be printed or aired without official consent. Even the title of this office was an exercise in seed planting. It was known as *The Ministry of Public Enlightenment and Propaganda*. The choice of the word "enlightenment" is interesting. I have always been a student of the etymology of words. How a word or concept develops meaning over time is quite a study. Take the word "propaganda" for instance. It comes from the word "propagate."

PROPAGATION

1. The breeding of plants or animals: *Our propagation of poppies is by seed, and of roses by cuttings.*
2. The handing down of qualities etc., in a family line.
3. Spreading; getting more widely believed; making more widely known: the propagation of the principles of science.
4. Passing on; sending further; spreading or extending: *The prop-*

agation of sound waves, the propagation of the shock of an earth-quake.

PROPAGANDIST

A person who gives time or effort in the spreading of some opinion, belief or principle.[1]

The idea is that *of dissemination* which means to spread seeds. It is in this sense that I can trace the hand of the Devil.

I began this book with a story about a ceremony in Canada where a group of New Age/Progressive activists "planted" a Peace Pole. (Interesting imagery.) For all of the lofty rhetoric, it had little to do with peace, and one of the organizations represented at that ceremony has emerged as a major player in the carbon offset scheme to gain control over world economies by means of environmental legislation.

The seed that was planted has, in a mere twenty-five years, sprouted into a movement heavily funded by the UN, and a handful of globalists who have become billionaires through manipulating the global warming scare. But something else was planted that day back in the little mountain town in British Columbia... the notion that any beliefs that run counter to a one-world, homogenized, green, all inclusive, non-confrontational religion, must be eliminated.

I remember thinking at the time I heard it, "No one would ever try to actually implement such a thing...not today." The public is too *enlightened* for that.

In 2011, I preached a message in a church in Canada. My good friend who hosted me that day commented on my message (at my invitation). I asked him how he thought the services went. He said it was fine, but added a sobering postscript. He paused and then said, "FYI. I should tell you that if anyone with a smart phone recorded one of your illustrations that referenced the gay agenda, and took offense and submitted it to the authorities, you could have been arrested for hate speech."

Just this last week a man *was* arrested in Great Britain for quoting a statement by no less a personage than Winston Churchill. Sir Winston once spoke in unflattering terms about the "Mohammedans." The scholar was citing a historical source and he was arrested. [2]

Do you really now think that if a pastor is doing a series of messages on "Family" and fails to speak in a positive fashion about gay marriage that he or she is not in danger of serious repercussions? Do you really think that the data mining by the NSC and use of the IRS as the punisher of political free speech will just suddenly stop because of the largesse of a politician?

Earlier In this book I cited Francis Schaeffer and the dire predictions he made in his book *The Great Evangelical Disaster*. You will remember that he predicted that if the seminaries continued to devalue the Word of God, and if progressive politics took hold in greater measure, the value of human life itself was in jeopardy. Perhaps you reacted at that point and thought "He (Schaeffer) is over-reacting."

Judge for yourselves the following news stories from early 2014. An Oregon newspaper, on New Year's Day, ran a feature article about an enterprising hipster who had written a cookbook with recipes for how to cook and eat the placenta after a baby is born. The article said "maybe a nice lasagna…a taco salad…or placenta chips…the possibilities are endless." The only objection raised in this article was not that this was part of the birth of a human being, it was that vegetarians and vegans might be conflicted. Was the placenta locally grown? [3]

The second story was actually reported fairly widely which makes the lack of outrage all the more disturbing. Abortion mills in Europe have figured out a way to ship the *products of the procedure* (aborted babies) to Canada and ultimately to Oregon *in order to be burned as fuel…in abortion clinics…to save the environment.*[4]

I have shown how the abandonment of trust in an inerrant Bible has had tragic consequences in seminaries. It is interesting that the word "seminary" comes from the same root as the word semen… or seed. The seminary is the place where seeds are planted and sprout and yield a theology and ultimately…a mindset.

Now in seminary you are liable to hear favorable lectures about the beauty of Islam, and be invited to have "conversations" about the new inclusive language to use when referring to the LGBT community. The best-selling Christian books are now touting the same notion that the COEXIST and HONOR DIVERSITY bumper stickers have been touting for years. We are all the same and essentially worshiping the same god. The president of one of the largest "new evangelical" seminaries in the world announces that he is going to celebrate Ramadan in solidarity with the Muslims, and the Christian media celebrate his progressive thinking.

A runaway bestseller builds its plotline around the notion of Universal Reconciliation…a spurious doctrine, long held to be heretical, that says in essence that no one is going to be lost and that the devil himself is going to be saved.[5]

Perhaps the most influential (in a political sense) pastor in the United Sates prays at the inauguration of the President a prayer in which he intentionally links the Jewish and Muslim and Christian names for Jesus, clearly inferring that they are the same person. Since then he has appeared at Muslim conventions and invited speakers who are sympathetic to the Palestinians to address his congregation. The term "Chrislam" is now in vogue some evangelical circles…and seminary professors write glowing reviews.

What are the implications of all of this for you and me? I tried to make the case that it is not outlandish to think that tyranny is at the door as our political leaders abandon any moral restraint in an ever-increasing progressive collectivist mindset. This will necessitate a one-world religious entity that has nothing to with biblical Christianity and everything to do with the elimination of religions that fail to embrace the New Age.

Let's return to the parable Jesus taught His disciples about the wheat and the tares. The tare' He referred to was most probably darnell… a false wheat…it looks like wheat and really doesn't appear to be the noxious weed that it is until it is full grown and mixed in with the full grown wheat.

His disciples asked Jesus about the meaning of the parable. Jesus said in no uncertain terms that it was not their responsibility to root out the weeds. He rightly concluded that good wheat would be lost if they tried to root out the tares in their own strength. In fact, when he explained the parable, He identified the tares as "the sons of the evil one…" not a doctrine…but actual people. And the only ones tasked with rounding them up were the angels (Matt. 13).

The good seeds are *the children of the kingdom*. What should the children of the kingdom do in times like these? Are we to become activists and bomb throwers? Are we to form a political party under the Christian banner? Are we to burn the books we disagree with? Absolutely not. But we are to push back every time the liar lies. We are not to just sit idly by as so called experts tell us that the Word of God is mere literature and that a new narrative is emerging, and that what we knew to be true has been exposed as mere mythology and literary device. No, we are to do some planting ourselves. In fact it is ourselves we must plant, taking action works when it is born of The Holy Spirit and done in love.

Recently the Christian relief agency World Vision shocked the church by announcing that the board of directors had lifted a previous sanction against same-sex couples participating in their ministry. In less than a week the board reversed their position and apologized.[7]

Why? What changed their minds?

The Church became the Church. A number of Christian leaders contacted World Vision and let them know that if they persisted in their position that denominations would begin to instruct their constituencies to not support World Vision any longer.

What a gut-wrenching decision. World Vision helps feed babies and starving people. Who would dare to oppose them on any grounds? Why, the leaders of the church who believe their Bibles, that's who. *Christianity Today* and other Christian media outlets bear some responsibility for their coverage of the whole debacle. Sympathetic articles appeared that gave the impression that World Vision was taking a bold but completely understandable position given the postmodern age in which we live.

It's time for a wake-up call. Remember that in the parable of the wheat and the tares Jesus said that planting of the tares took place *"When men were asleep."*

In this book I talked about the significance of:

- The Watershed

- The dangerous momentum of the Great Down Grade
- The critical need for restored trust in a reliable instrument
- The need to restore the whole notion of vetting leaders and authors
- And finally the need for a clear call back to the Bible.

I can't speak for you, but here is what I am doing. In 2013 I began a ministry called *The Jude 3 Evangelistic Association.*

Once this book is released in the fall of 2014, *The Jude Evangelistic Association* will begin to network with like-minded pastors, theologians, and denominational officials as well as Christians in the workplace who are convinced about the truth of the message of this book. I personally will use such time as I have left on this earth to call the Church back to a place of trust in the reliability of the Scriptures. I will push back every time I read an article or hear a message that downplays the trustworthiness of the Bible. I will educate anyone who will listen about the inroads that progressives have made in the Church. I am literally going to travel the nation and contact pastors. My colleagues will offer seminars on:

- The inerrancy of Scripture
- How to interpret Scripture the old way
- How to push back against progressive propaganda.

I called it the Jude 3 Evangelistic Association because the message in verse three of Jude is what this book has been all about, and with it I conclude,

"Beloved, when I gave all diligence to write unto to you of the common salvation, it was needful for me to write unto you and exhort you that you should earnestly contend for the faith which was once for all delivered unto the saints."

The cover of this book depicts a ship about to break up on the rocks. Is there any remedy for a ship that has lost its anchor? Yes, but it must begin with a ruthless honesty and the humility to admit that something is very, very wrong.

Next a course correction must be made immediately. The instruments must be consulted. If the instruments themselves are reporting false data then scrap the instruments and go to the most primitive reckoning possible. Find the Morning Star and start from there. Decide on the non-negotiable, fixed starting point from which to plot your course. Mariners have referred to this as the "celestial fix."

Perhaps the hymn writer had it right after all.

In every high and stormy gale

My anchor holds within the veil.

On Christ the solid rock I stand

All other ground is shifting sand

All other ground is shifting sand.[8]

NOTES

INTRODUCTION

1. J.B. Cowman, *Streams in the Desert,* (Grand Rapids: Zondervan, 1997).
2. The Melodyland School of Theology, founded by Dr. Ralph Wilkerson was where I learned from notable faculty members such as Dr. J. Rodman Williams, Walter Martin, Dr. John Warwick Montgomery, Dr. Robert Frost, Dr. Ron Cottle and others.
3. Op. cit., *Streams in the Desert* quote.

CHAPTER 1

1. "World Peace University in Salmon Arm," *Shuswap Sun,* October 1, 1990.
2. Ibid.
3. The rationale for the course appears on the George Fox Website [georgefox.edu] "Why are we doing this?
   • The Earth is endangered.
   • The evangelical Church has been silent.
   • The Bible speaks to our relationship with the Created Order.
   • The Church must respond to God's command to "keep" the earth (Gen. 2:15).
   • Christian leaders need a theological and biblical basis for Earth-keeping.
4. Lucis Trust was originally called Lucifer Publishing. This bit of information is nowhere to be found on its current website, lucistrust.org. It is, however, listed as being, "on the Roster of the United Nations Economic and Social Council."
5. The mythical Gaia was the primal Greek goddess personifying the Earth, the Greek version of Mother Nature or the Earth Mother. The so-called Gaia hypothesis suggests that organisms co-evolve with their environment: that is, they "influence their abiotic environment, and that environment in turn influences the biota by Darwinian process." Lovelock [1995].

6. The World Economic Forum and religious leaders like Rick Warren and Brian McClaren are sympathetic to the initiatives of leaders from around the planet to work towards an interfaith approach to global governance.
7. Centering, breathing techniques, the use of religious icons, walking labyrinths, mystic mediation practices, are now fairly commonplace in spiritual formation programs.
8. Paul Smith, *New Evangelicalism: The New World* Order, (California, Calvary, 2011), 73.
9. Ibid.
10. Ibid.
11. Ibid.
12. Warren B. Smith, "Are Christian and Emerging Leaders Heading Toward a False Christ Through Quantum Spirituality?" (*Lighthouse Trails*, July 11, 2009).
13. Ibid.
14. Ibid.
15. Ibid.
16. The *Sushwap Sun* article's description of The World Peace University goals are very similar to Frijof Capra's.
17. George Russell, "Exclusive: Godfather of Global Green Steps Out of Shadows at Rio + 12" (Fox News, June 20, 2012, accessed December 15, 2012), http://www.foxnews.com/world/2012/06/20/godfather-global-green-thinking-steps-out-shadows-at-rio-20/#ixzz29O8PgEOZ.
18. Ibid.
19. Claudia Rosett, "The UN's Man of Mystery" (*The Wall Street Journal*, October 22, 2008, accessed December 15, 2012), http://online.wsj.com/article/SB122368007369524679.html.
20. "I am the Lord Thy God which have brought thee out of the land of Egypt, out of the house of bondage, Thou Shalt have no other Gods before Me" (Exodus 20…The Ten Commandments). I can think of no instance in Scripture where believers are enjoined to study and understand other religions. I can find plenty of injunctions against

believers attempting to join in the worship of other gods.

CHAPTER 2

1. Wikipedia, "Columbia River" (September 10, 2012), accessed September 19, 2012, http://en.wikipedia.org/wiki/Columbia_River.
2. Francis A. Schaeffer, *The Great Evangelical Disaster,* (Westchester: Crossway, 1984), 44.
3. Ibid, 45.
4. Ibid, 60.
5. Ibid, 62.
6. Ibid, 22.
7. Ibid, 23.
8. Saul Hubbard, "Planned Parenthood sets its roots," (*The Register Guard,* September 29, 2012, accessed December 15, 2012), http://projects.registerguard.com/web/newslocalnews/26951241-41/parenthood-planned-glenwood-center-springfield.html.csp.
9. The Op Ed I submitted never appeared.
10. It is an eye opening experience to research Planned Parenthood Founder Margaret Sanger's ties to the eugenics movement.
11. Francis A. Schaeffer, *The Great Evangelical Disaster,* (Westchester: Crossway, 1984), 101.
12. Ibid.
13. Denny Burk, "McLaren Presides over Same-Sex Commitment Ceremony" (DennyBurk.com, September 25, 2012, accessed December 15, 2012), http://www.dennyburk.com/mclaren-presides-over-same-sex-commitment-ceremony/.
14. Francis A. Schaeffer, *The Great Evangelical Disaster,* (Westchester: Crossway, 1984), 150.

CHAPTER 3

1. Dennis M. Swanson, "The Down Grade Controversy and Evangelical Boundaries: Some Lessons from Spurgeon's Battle for Evangelical Orthodoxy," (Colorado Springs: Evangelical Theological Society, 2001).

2. Andrew Perriman, "Open Source Technology," *Emergingchurch.info*, February 2012, accessed September 4, 2012, http://www.emergingchurch.info/reflection/ andrewperriman/index.htm.

3. Charles Spurgeon, "Another Word Concerning the Downgrade," *The Sword and the Trowell* (Pasadena, Pilgrim, August 23, 1887), 195.

4. Dennis M. Swanson, "The Down-grade Controversy and Evangelical Boundaries: Some Lessons from Spurgeon's Battle for Evangelical Orthodoxy," (Colorado Springs: Evangelical Theological Society, 2001), 25.

5. John MacArthur, "Seminary Graduation," *Grace to You.* May 11, 2007, accessed September 4, 2012,
   http://www.gty.org/resources/sermons/80-170/seminary-graduation.

6. Ibid.

7. Ibid.

8. Dr. W.A. Criswell, "Whether We Live or Die," spoken at the Southern Baptist Convention (Dallas, Texas, June 10, 1985).

9. Ibid.

10. C.H. Mackintosh, *Miscellaneous Writings,* (New York: Jehoshaphat, 1975).

11. Robert Frost's The Road Not Taken www.poetryfoundation.org › Poems & Poets.

CHAPTER 4:

1. Donald A. McGavran, *The Bridges of God* ,(Scribd, accessed October 9, 2012), 1981. http://www.scribd.com/doc/69104106/mcgavran-the-bridges.

2. Paul Smith, *New Evangelicalism: The New World Order*, p.101.

3. Ibid., 75.

4. Ibid., 109-110.

CHAPTER 5:

1. Phyllis Tickle's book is entitled *The Great Emergence: How Christianity Is Changing and Why.*
   "Tickle's basic thesis is that every 500 years, the Church goes through

a rummage sale, and cleans out the old forms of spirituality and replaces it with new ones. This does *not* mean that previous forms become obsolete or invalid. It simply means they lose *pride of place* as the dominant form of Christianity. Constantine in the late 4th century, early 5th, the Great Schism of the 11th century, the Reformation in the 16th century, and now the Postmodern era in the 21st century have all been points of reference for these changes.

What is giving way right now is Protestantism, in the form that we know it, and what is emerging is a new form of Christianity, what she is calling "The Great Emergence." One can only guess whether or not it is tribal form, an individualistic form, a social form, or a combination of all of them. But, what we can say is that Protestantism in all its denominational forms is losing influence and is giving way to alternative forms of Christian expression."

http://vialogue.wordpress.com/2008/04/27/the-great-emergence-phyllis-tickles-500-year-rummage-sale/.

2. PBS, "Postmodern," accessed December 15, 2012,
http://www.pbs.org/faithandreason/gengloss/postm-body.html.

3. The *New International Commentary on The New Testament -The Book of Revelation* by Robert H. Mounce, (Wm. B Eerdmans Publishing Company Grand Rapids, Michigan, 1997 [note on chap. 2:6]).

4. Ibid., p.89.

5. Ibid., pp.97–98.

6. Ibid., p.103.

7. Ibid., p.103.

8. Mignon Fogarty, "What is a Canard?" (Grammar Girl, December 16, 2010, accessed October 9, 2012),
http://grammar.quickanddirtytips.com/what-is-a-canard.aspx.

9. See Greek definition in *Strong's Concordance* on the word 'blinded'… [2 Corinthians 4:4] *tuphlos.*

10. David Dunlap, "Donald Miller and Blue Like Jazz" (Bible & Life, Bible Teaching Newsletter, Vol. 15 No. 1, January 1, 2008).

11. Ibid.

12. Ibid.

13. Ibid.

14. Ibid.

15. See James De Young's book, *Burning Down the Shack*, (WND Books, Published by World Net Daily, Washington, D.C. 2010, Introduction, pp. ix and x).

16. NBC Olympics Coverage/Women's Marathon Swim 2012.

17. Gay Talese, *The Bridge,* (Ontario: Walker Publishing Company, 2003).

18. Robert Frost, *Mending Wall*
http://www.poemhunter.com/poem/mending-wall/.

CHAPTER 6:

1. Gina Harkins, "Navigating by a compass in the age of GPS? Why bother?" (*Marine Corps Times*, July 5, 2012).

2. Bryce C.K. Muhlenberg, Marine Corps.

3. Gina Harkins, "Navigating by a compass in the age of GPS? Why bother?" (*Marine Corps Times*, July 5, 2012).

4. Roy Hicks and Margaret Hicks, *Ready or Not, Here Come Trouble,* (Oklahoma: Harrison, 1980) 9.

5. Ibid, 12–13.

6. Ibid, 14.

7. Ibid, 10.

8. J.I. Packer, "The Approach to Biblical Interpretation" (accessed December 15, 2012), http://www.ccel.us/packer.ch4.html.

CHAPTER 7:

1. Leonard Sweet, *Quantum Spirituality,* Dayton, Ohio: United Theological Seminary, 1991), 10.

2. Class notes from Dr. Montgomery's lectures at Melodyland School of Theology.

3. Leonard Sweet, *Quantum Spirituality,* Dayton, Ohio: United Theological Seminary, 1991), 191.

4. Ibid., 53.

5. Ibid.

6. Ibid.

7. *Strong's Greek Dictionary of The New Testament, hupotuposis.*

8. Tom Roberts, "Rightly Divide the Word of Truth" (Watchman Mag, June 2001) accessed December 15, 2012, http://www.watchmanmag.com/0406indx.htm.

9. *Land Navigation Handbook*, Marine Barracks, Washington, D.C.

10. Netfax, "Advertising Joins the Journey of the Soul" (Leadernet Number 74, June 23, 1997).

CHAPTER 8:

1. F.F. Bruce, *Commentary on Paul's Epistles to the Colossians, Philemon and Ephesians: The New International Commentary on the New Testament* (Grand Rapids: Wm B. Eerdmans, 1984).

2. Wikipedia, "Lockheed EC-130H Compass Call" (October 21, 2012) accessed December 15, 2012, http://en.wikipedia.org/wiki/Compass_Call.

3. Post-Structuralism, Wikipedia (updated December 30, 2012, accessed January 6, 2013), http://en.wikipedia.org/wiki/Post-structuralism.

4. Emmanuel Levinas, *Humanism of the Other,* (Chicago: University of Illinois Press, 2003), 11–12.

5. Wikipedia, "Jean-Francois Lyotard" (December 11, 2012, accessed December 15, 2012), http://en.wikipedia.org/wiki/Jean-Francois_Lyotard.

6. J.R. Daniel Kirk, "Wikipedia, "Roland Barthes" (December 15, 2012, accessed December 15, 2012), http://en.wikipedia.org/wiki/Roland_Barthes.

7. Narrative Theology and Transformed Meaning" (Storied Theology, February 25, 2012, accessed October 10, 2012), http://www.jrdkirk.com/2012/02/25/narrative-theology-and-transformed-meaning/.

8. Ibid.

9. J.M. Balkin, *Cultural Software: A Theory of Ideology* (London: Yale University, 1998).

10. Ibid.

11. Ibid.

12. Ibid.

13. Desmond Alexander, "Is there a wedge being driven between Biblical Theology and Systematic Theology?" (Biblical Theology, Word Press, November 2008) accessed December 15, 2012, http://biblicaltheology.wordpress.com/2008/11/11/is-there-a-wedge-being-driven-between-biblical-theology-and-systematic-theology/.

CHAPTER 9:

1. James B. DeYoung, *Burning Down The Shack,* (WND Publishing, Washington D.C., 2010).

2. I met with Dr. DeYoung on two occasions. His research and person knowledge of the origins of *The Shack* are invaluable. William Paul Young definitely set out to push the doctrine of Universal Reconciliation despite his protestations to the contrary.

3. See http://www.answers.com/topic/vetting for a more thorough treatment of the etymology of the term.

4. Ibid.

CHAPTER 10:

1. Francis A. Schaeffer, *The Great Evangelical Disaster* (Westchester: Crossway, 1984), 19.

2. Ibid., 20.

3. Ibid., 20.

4. Ibid., 21.

5. Ibid., 23.

6. Ibid., 23.

7. Ibid., 33.

8. Ibid., 34.

9. Ibid., 35.

10. Ibid., 35.id., 37.

11. *Time* Magazine Cover July 4, 2011 Richard Stengel wrote the accompanying article.

12. Schaeffer op. cit., pp. 50–52.

13. "Why Obamacare could result in early deaths of millions of baby

boomers" (*Whistleblower* Single Issue Magazine, August 2009, accessed September 20, 2012),

http://www.wnd.com/2009/09/105872.

14. Ibid.
15. Ibid.
16. Ibid.
17. Ibid.
18. Ibid.
19. I sent this for publication but it was never printed.
20. T.L. Green, "The Negro Project: Margaret Sanger Eugenic Plan for Black Americans" (Citizen Review, May 10, 2001, accessed September 20, 1012),

http://www.citizenreviewonline.org/special_issues/population/the_negro_project.htm.
21. Ibid.
22. Ibid.
23. Ibid.
24. Inge Scholl, *The White Rose: Munich 1942-1943* (Middleton: Wesleyan University, 1983), 42.
25. Ibid.
26. Ibid.

CHAPTER 11

1. The United States Holocaust Memorial Museum, *White Rose* (May 22, 2012, accessed January 6, 2013),

http://www.ushmm.org/wlc/en/article.php?ModuleId=10007188.
2. Inge Scholl, *The White Rose: Munich 1942-1943* (Middleton: Wesleyan University, 1983), 9.
3. Ibid., 17.
4. Ibid., 20.
5. Ibid., 24–25.
6. Ibid.
7. See drjamesdobson.org for a lengthy description of what led him to a position of such strident opposition to the president

http://drjamesdobson.org/about/commentaries/the-truth-about-life.

8. Jonathan Merritt, *A Faith of Our Own-Following Jesus Beyond the Culture Wars* (New York: Faith Words, 2012), 77.

9. Ibid., 57.

10. Ibid., 161–162.

11. Ibid., 145–146.

12. Ibid., 122.

13. Ibid., 89.

14. Ibid.

CHAPTER 12

1. Eric, Metaxas, *Bonhoeffer,* (Nashville: Thomas Nelson, 2010. Print).

2. Ibid., 105.

3. Ibid., 107.

4. Ibid., 165.

5. Ibid., 171.

6. Ibid., 173.

7. Ibid., 175.

8. Ibid.

9. Ibid.

10. United States Holocaust Memorial Museum, "Martin Niemöller: 'First they came for the Socialists...'" (May 12, 2012, accessed December 15, 2012),
    http://www.ushmm.org/wlc/en/article.php?ModuleId=10007392.

11. Eric, Metaxas, *Bonhoeffer,* (Nashville: Thomas Nelson, 2010).

12. Ibid.

13. Ibid., 190.

14. L. Gaussen, D.D., *Theopneustia: The Plenary Inspiration of the Holy Scripture,* (London: Johnstone & Hunter, 1850), 146.

CHAPTER 13

1. Francis A. Schaeffer, *The Great Evangelical Disaster,* (Westchester: Crossway, 1984), 83.

2. Ibid.

3. Ibid.

4. Erwin Lutzer, *Hitler's Cross,* (Chicago: Moody Publishers, 1995).

5. Ibid.

6. This congress took place subsequent to the Salmon Arm Peace Pole Ceremony cited in Chapter One.

7. Ibid.

8. Bill Clinton, "The Case for Optimism," (*Time* Magazine, October 2012).

9. Ibid.

10. Ibid.

11. Jaweed Kaleem, "Rick Warren, Saddleback Pastor: Obama Has 'Infringed' Upon Religious Liberties" (*Huffington Post*, November 28, 2012, accessed December 15, 2012),
    http://www.huffingtonpost.com/2012/11/28/rick-warren-obama-religious-liberty_n_2206064.html.

12. Michael Gryboski, "Rick Warren Says President Obama 'Infringed' on Religious Liberties" (*The Christian Post*, November 29, 2012, accessed December 15, 2012),
    http://m.christianpost.com/news/rick-warren-says-president-obama-infringed-on-religious-liberties-85797/.

13. L.W. Munhall, *Anti-Higher Criticism,* (New York City: Hunt & Eaton, 1843-1934).

14. Ibid.

15. Guidepost.

16. World Net Daily, "Atheists Claim Ground Zero Cross Sickens Them" (October 18, 2012, accessed December 15, 2012),
    http://www.wnd.com/2012/08/atheists-claim-ground-zero-cross-sickens-them/.

17. Munhall, *Anti-Higher Criticism.*

Chapter 14

1. John Warrick Montgomery, *God's Inerrant Word: An International Symposium on the Trustworthiness of Scripture,* (Minneapolis: Bethany Fellowship, 1974), 15.

2. Ibid., 17–18.

3. Ibid., 38.

4. Ibid., 39.

5. Ibid.

6. Guy P. Duffield and Nathaniel M. Van Cleave, *Foundations of Pentecostal Theology,* (Los Angeles: L.I.F.E Bible College, 1983), 18.

7. Ibid., 25.

8. Jeff Kunerth, "UCF professor Charles Negy challenges America's 'religious bigotry,'" (*The Vindicator,* September 15, 2012).

9. Ibid.

10. Paul Smith, *New Evangelicalism: The New World Order* (California: Calvary, 2011), 15.

11. Ibid., 35.

12. *Strong's Exhaustive Concordance,* Hebrew Dictionary on the word "Horonite" [Khoor].

13. Read more: http://newsbusters.org/blogs/brent-baker/2013/01/18/newsweek-makes-it-official-obama-s-inauguration-second-coming#ixzz2ImLT3Cbn.

14. Fox News/Jon Scot interview Jan. 22, 2013.

15. The O'Reilly Factor coverage of Sec'y Clinton's testimony Jan. 23, 2013.

16. For this quote see http://www.corsinet.com/braincandy/qtruth.html.

17. Ibid.

EPILOGUE

1. *Thorndike & Barnhart Junior Dictionary,* Scott, Foresmen and Company, Chicago 1962, (entries for words *Propagation* and *Propagandist),* p.525.

2. Selwyn Duke, "Hate speech: U.K. Political Leader Arrested for Quoting Winston Churchill," www.thenewamerican.com April 29, 2014.

3. Placenta recipe books are now available on Amazon.com http://www.amazon.com/25-Placenta-Recipes-Delicious-placenta-ebook/dp/B00BN2JP78.

4. This article references the practice in the U.K which has since been adopted in Canada. Ultimately some of the fetuses to be burned for fuel to heat abortion mills have found their way to Oregon http://www.telegraph.co.uk/health/healthnews/10717566/Aborted-babies-incinerated-to-heat-UK-hospitals.html.

5. In his book *The Shack* (originally Windblown Media, from mid-2008 with FaithWords, the Christian division of Hachette Book Group USA [Hodder & Stoughton for UK] Publication date May, 2007), William Paul Young is voicing support for a doctrine known as Universal Reconciliation. A colleague of his at the time, (they were in a study group together) Dr. James DeYoung confronted Young and has written a powerful rebuttal in his book, *Burning Down "The Shack": How the "Christian" Bestseller Is Deceiving Millions,* WND Books; 1st edition (June 1, 2010).

   Perhaps most troubling of all is when Christians who have read *The Shack* are confronted with this indisputable evidence of Young's intentional attempt to change how the God of the Bible is portrayed, they often tend to say things like, "But it made me feel so good."

6. There was an initially favorable treatment of World Vision's policy by *Christianity Today*. After the firestorm of outrage, *Christianity Today* took a more benign, objective stance. http://spectator.org/blog/58529/world-vision-backs-down.

7. http://lutheran-hymnal.com/lyrics/tlh370.htm The lyrics to *On Christ the Solid Rock I Stand,* written by Edward Mote.

Bibliography

Barthes, Roland. "The Death of the Author." Tbook. N.p., n.d. Web. 04 Sept. 2012.

Bawer, Bruce. While Europe Slept. New York: Doubleday, 2006. Print.

Bible-translation-screenplay-format-085746946.html>.

Blumhofer, Edith L. Aimee Semple McPherson: *Everybody's Sister*. Grand Rapids: William B. Eerdmans, 1993. Print.

Bruce, F.F. Commentary on the Book of Acts. Grand Rapids: WM. B. Eerdmans, 1979. Print.

Criswell, W.A., Dr. "Whether We Live or Die." Southern Baptist Convention. Dallas, Texas. 10 June 1985. Speech.

De Young, James B. *Burning Down 'The Shack'*. Washington D.C.: WND, 2010. Print.

DeWaay, Bob. "Emergent Delusion: A Critique of Brian McLaren, a Generous Orthodoxy." *Critical Issues Commentary.* N.p., Mar. 2005. Web. 04 Sept. 2012. <http://cicministry.org/commentary/ issue 87.htm>.

Diekmann, Scott. "How the 'Fates' of Pastor Todd Wilken and Leonard Sweet Are Related." The Wittenberg Trail. Norm Fisher, 24 Mar. 2008. Web. 04 Sept. 2012. <http://wittenbergtrail.org/profiles/blogs/1453099:BlogPost:61525>.

D'Souza, Dinesh. What's so Great about Christianity. New York: MJF, 2007. Print.

Duffield, Guy P., and Nathaniel M. Van. Foundations of Pentecostal Theology. Los Angeles: L.I.F.E Bible College, 1983. Print.

"For Emergence Christianity out Goes the Bible and in Comes 'Queer Christians.'" Watcher's Lamp. Blogspot, 12 Dec. 2008. Web. 04 Sept. 2012. <http://watcherslamp.blogspot.com/2008/12/emergents-trading-sola-scriptura-for.html>.

Hicks, Roy, and Margaret Hicks. Ready or Not, Here Come Trouble. Oklahoma: Harrison, 1980. Print.

Hunt, Dave, and T.A. McMahon. The Seduction of Christianity: Spiritual Discernment in the Last Days. N.p.: Harvest, 1985. Print.

Karen. "Spurgeon Quotes on Apostasy." Girded with Truth. N.p., 22 Feb. 2012. Web. 04 Sept. 2012.

<http://www.girdedwithtruth.org/?s=spurgeon+quotes+on+apostasy>.

Leber, Annedore, comp. Conscience in Revolt. N.p.: Vallentine Mitchell, 1957. Print.

Lewis, C. S. The Last Battle. New York: Collier, 1956. Print.

Lindsell, Harold. The Battle for the Bible. N.p.: Zondervan, 1976. Print.

Loller, Travis. "New Bible Translation Has Screenplay Format." Yahoo! Finance. Yahoo!, 30 July 2012. Web. 04 Sept. 2012. <http://finance. yahoo.com/news/.

MacArthur, John. Seminary Graduation. Grace to You. N.p., 11 May 2007. Web. 04 Sept. 2012. <http://www.gty.org/resources/sermons/80-170/seminary-graduation>.

MacArthur, John. The Truth War. Nashville: Thomas Nelson, 2007. Print.

Marshall, I. Howard, et al., eds. New Bible Dictionary. 3rd ed. Leicester: Inter-Varsity, 1996. Print.

Martindale, Wayne, and Jerry Root, eds. The Quotable Lewis. Wheaton: Tyndale, 1989. Print.

McCasland, David. Oswald Chambers: Abandoned to God. N.p.: Discovery, 1993. Print.

McKnight, Scot. "Five Streams of the Emerging Church." Christian Today. N.p., 19 Jan. 2007. Web. 04 Sept. 2012. <http://www.christianityto-day.com/ct/2007/february/11.35.html>.

Note: Scot McKnight's blog, "Jesus Creed" has many posts on the Emerging Movement. His older blogs include "Divine Hours Daily Blog" and "Jesus and His Death." He has also written "The Mary We Never Knew" for Christian Today. Christian Today has a special "Emergence for Emergent" section.

Metaxas, Eric. Bonhoeffer. Nashville: Thomas Nelson, 2010. Print.

Montgomery, John Warrick. God's Inerrant Word: An International Symposium on the Trustworthiness of Scripture. N.p.: Bethany Fellowship, 1974. Print.

Morris, Audrey Stone, comp. One Thousand Inspirational Things. New York: Spencer, 1936. Print.

Munhall, L.V. "The Integrity and Authority of the Bible." The New York City Methodist Preacher's Meeting. New York City. 17 Apr. 1899. Address.

Munhall, L.W. The Highest Critics Vs. The Highest Critics. 3rd ed. New York: Hunt & Eaton, 1896. Print.

Perrimen, Andrew. "Open Source Technology." Emergingchurch.info. N.p., 4 Feb. 2012. Web. 04 Sept. 2012. <http://www.emergingchurch.info/reflection/andrewperriman/index.htm>.

Schaeffer, Francis A. The Great Evangelical Disaster. Westchester: Crossway, 1984. Print.

Sproul, R.C. Scripture Alone: The Evangelical Doctrine. N.p.: P&R, 2005. Print.

Swanson, Dennis M. "The Down-grade Controversy and Evangelical Boundaries: Soem Lessons from Spurgeon's Battle for Evangelical Orthodoxy." Evangelical Theological Society. Colorado Springs. Nov. 2001. Reading.

White, Heath. Post-Modernism 101. Grand Rapids: Brazos, 2006. Print.

CONTACT THE AUTHOR
Dr. Jim Jenkins is available for speaking engagements and
in-service training events.
The Jude 3 Evangelistic Association
PO Box 667
Monmouth, OR 97361

To learn more about Fatal Drift, or
to contact the author please visit:
www.fataldrift.com